DATE DUE

DEMCO 38-296

Pioneers of Early Childhood Education

Pioneers of Early Childhood Education

A BIO-BIBLIOGRAPHICAL GUIDE

Barbara Ruth Peltzman

GREENWOOD PRESS
Westport, Connecticut • London

Library of Congress Cataloging-in-Publication Data

Peltzman, Barbara R., 1946–
    Pioneers of early childhood education : a bio-bibliographical
guide / Barbara Ruth Peltzman.
        p.   cm.
    Includes index.
    ISBN 0–313–30404–1 (alk. paper)
    1. Early childhood education—Bio-bibliography.   2. Early
childhood educators—Biography.   I. Title.
LB1139.23.P45   1998
372.21′092′2—dc21   97–26907

British Library Cataloguing in Publication Data is available.

Library of Congress Catalog Card Number: 97–26907
ISBN: 0–313–30404–1

First published in 1998

Greenwood Press, 88 Post Road West, Westport, CT 06881
An imprint of Greenwood Publishing Group, Inc.

Printed in the United States of America

The paper used in this book complies with the
Permanent Paper Standard issued by the National
Information Standards Organization (Z39.48–1984).

10 9 8 7 6 5 4 3

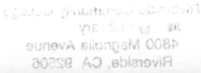

To the memory of my uncle Leon J. Miln,
a pioneer in many ways.

Pioneers! O Pioneers!
Conquering, holding, daring, venturing as we
go the unknown ways.
Pioneers! O Pioneers!

Walt Whitman

To know what is possible tomorrow you must be willing
to step outside of what is possible today...

Ralph Waldo Emerson

Contents

Preface

The educators who built the field of early childhood education have been the subject of many studies including Agnes Snyder's 1972 book, *Dauntless Women in Childhood Education, 1856-1931,* and the 1992 ACEI sequel, *Profiles in Childhood Education, 1931-1960.* Previous works, however, do not provide the researcher with primary and secondary sources, information on multicultural educators, nor do they discuss some of the more current educators. Researchers and practitioners frequently need to locate material that is only available in primary sources. They also may want to know what someone else thinks about a method or theory so that there can be a meeting of the minds to help with a decision.

Millie Almy (1984) believes that everyone involved with the present and future of the education of young children needs to make judgments about educational trends in light of knowledge about theory and practice. One way to assist researchers and practitioners to make informed decisions is to provide an annotated bibliography of primary and secondary sources in early childhood education. This reference book provides biographies and bibliographies of selected pre-modern and modern men and women who have made significant contributions to early childhood education. Individuals and organizations, for example the National Association of Colored Women, were selected because they represent a multicultural perspective on early childhood education. The biographies provide a personal perspective in which to view the primary sources. Information about the pioneers helps the reader to understand the theories and practices discussed in the context of the times in which they were written.

It is impossible to include everything by and about every pioneer. However, the material presented in this resource provides a perspective on each important era in the history of early childhood education.

The biographies are arranged in alphabetical order followed by the primary sources arranged in chronological order. Secondary sources are listed alphabetically according to author and include obituaries, articles, dissertations, and books. Works were chosen because they represent the most interesting and informative sources by and about the pioneers.

The work of the pioneers have influenced, as Bernard Spodek (1973) states, "current practice in early childhood education. For each, education developed out of...a humanist tradition, a concern for young children, for the support of their autonomy and development, and a belief in the importance of the early experiences in the lives of people." It is vital to study the past because, as Spodek informs us, there are "striking parallels between historical and contemporary theory and practice." We know that there is very little that is new in education. Time has shown that much of what contemporary theorists and practitioners discover, has its roots in the past. Spodek, Saracho, and Davis (1991) support this: "if we are to understand the field of early childhood education...we must know...of its historical roots and development." Theory and practice respond to contemporary concerns but "a perspective on the past provides a keener awareness of the multiple possibilities for the instruction and guidance of children."

This book attempts to illuminate the recent and distant past of early childhood education and, it is hoped, that "future scholars will benefit from the research and will help to recognize" [many more educators who contribute] "to the education of (young) children" (Meyer, 1992).

REFERENCES

ACEI Later Leaders Committee. *Profiles in Childhood Education, 1931-1960.* Washington, D.C.: Association for Childhood Education International, 1992.

Adams, Olga. "Foreword," In *Dauntless Women in Childhood Education, 1856-1931,* by Agnes Snyder. Washington, D.C.: Association for Childhood Education International, 1972.

Almy, Millie. "Foreword," In *Ideas Influencing Early Childhood Education: A Theoretical Analysis,* by Evelyn Weber. New York: Teachers College Press, 1984.

Meyer, Alberta L. "Foreword," In *Profiles in Childhood Education, 1931-1960,* by ACEI. Later Leaders Committee. Washington, D.C.: Association for Childhood Education International, 1992.

Snyder, Agnes. *Dauntless Women in Childhood Education, 1856-1931.* Washington, D.C.: Association for Childhood Education International, 1972.

Spodek, Bernard. *Early Childhood Education.* New Jersey: Prentice-Hall, 1972.

Spodek, Bernard, Olivia Saracho, and Michael Davis. *Foundations of Early Childhood Education: Teaching Three, Four, and Five Year Old Children.* New Jersey: Prentice-Hall, 1991.

Acknowledgments

Many kind and supportive colleagues have assisted in the completion of this book in countless ways. Professor Lois Cherepon and Professor Sandra Math, reference librarians at the Loretto Memorial Library, St. John's University, were able to track down obscure material and always found what was needed. Carmella Tino, reference librarian at the St. John's University Library, Queens Campus, located many needed sources. Marcia Moss, reference librarian and Municipal Archivist at the Concord Free Public Library in Concord, Massachusetts, provided time and help in locating material on William Torrey Harris. Martin Knorr, Archivist at the Harris-Stowe State College in St. Louis, provided material by and about William Torrey Harris. Olivia Aguilar Gattis, Archivist at the National Education Association, helped locate nineteenth-century *NEA Proceedings.*

Professor Lauren Brown, Curator of Historical Manuscripts and Archivist of the University of Maryland ACEI Archives, and his staff, especially Phyllis Waters, provided guidance and material on the International Kindergarten Union, and many pioneers. The Public Information departments of the National Association for the Education of Young Children and the Association for Childhood Education International provided reprints, friendly words, and direction. Beth Alberty of the Workshop Center on Open Education was generous with her time, sharing personal memories of Lillian Weber and material from her work in progress. Susan Kaler and Judy Ceven of the Wheelock College Library provided time and material on Lucy Wheelock which could not be found elsewhere. Dr. Earl Bean of the Huntington Library, Hampton University, provided information from the archives. Wendy Thomas, Public Service Librarian at the Schlesinger Library, Radcliffe College, provided help, printouts, and time. Roland Baumann, Archivist at Oberlin College, provided information on women graduates and the kindergarten at Oberlin.

Elisabeth Ogilvie and Dorothy Simpson were generous with their encouragement. Dr. Midred Dougherty of William Patterson College, editor of the *Reading Instruction Journal of the NJRA,* provided support and advice. D. Keith Osborn of the University of Georgia shared his research and provided encouragement until his untimely death in 1994. Dr. Dorothy Hewes, historian and professor emeritus of San Diego State University and OMEP, shared her knowledge, research, and insights on William Hailman, Elizabeth Palmer Peabody, and many hard to find sources.

There are dozens of reference librarians and archivists who were voices on the phone and they were a great help in many ways.

Moral support was provided by Dr. Irene S. Pyszkowski who encouraged, supported, and enjoyed this research from the start; Dr. Grace M. Dondero who encouraged, listened, and always found something at which to smile; and Dr. Teresa

A. Trimarco, chairperson and friend who gave generously of her precious time, listened, encouraged, and advised from the very start. She has given wisdom and provided direction.

Mrs. Irene Harris-Maken served as historical advisor and Mrs. Doris Roseman provided long distance encouragement. Dr. George Butler provided insight and expert editorial assistance. Mrs. Meg Fergusson provided expert copy editing and advice. Dianne DiBlasi did proofreading. And Joan Robelen did a masterful job of word-processing, proofreading, and page design.

My parents William and Norma Peltzman lived with the project daily, listened, advised, encouraged, and tolerated.

All of these people and many others deserve thanks and, to paraphrase Lawrence Cremin, credit for whatever worth the book may have. I, however, am responsible for its faults.

Introduction

The principles and practices of modern early childhood education have their origins in the past. As Evelyn Weber (1984) states, "contemporary theory has its roots in the past in a very real sense. In education tradition lingers long; ideas from the past intermingle with newer insights."

One of the founders of modern early childhood education is Johann Amos Comenius, a Moravian bishop who believed in social reform through education. His "General Postulates of Teaching and Learning," which appeared in his book *The Great Didactic* (1657), can be considered one of the first descriptions of a system of education designed specifically for young children. Comenius advocated learning through the senses by direct experience because sense impressions would be internalized and stored for future interpretation. According to Curtis and Boultwood (1961), Comenius believed that "the acquisition of knowledge is essentially based on activity followed by reasoning." Rudolph and Cohen (1964) apply Comenius' idea to kindergarten curriculum: "only by building on what the senses contact, will the child be ready for the symbolic learning that will come in time." We provide the experiences that children store for an understanding of concepts they will encounter later.

Comenius believed in education for all regardless of gender or social standing because, as Randolph Pounds (1968) states, his was a ladder system in which all children would "take the same route and would ... stop at different levels." Comenius also believed in individual differences among children. As Keating (1921) translates, "the same method cannot be applied to all alike. Each one will develop in the direction of his natural inclinations." His system of education was divided into four levels, from infancy to adulthood, outlining the types of educational experiences required at each stage of development from "the School of the Mother's Knee," using nursery school and kindergarten methods, to university and travel for the youth and adult. This division of the educational experience with recognition of the special needs of young children was new. Other scholars built on the work done by Comenius to further the concept of early education.

Jean-Jacques Rousseau advocated naturalism in education, believing that children were good if they were raised away from the evils of society. According to Bayles and Hood (1966), Rousseau believed that if a child were protected from society, his/her own "innate tendencies would have the opportunity to grow and unfold in accordance with its own nature."

In order to allow children to grow and learn naturally, Rousseau envisioned a system of education radically different from the prevailing practices. *Émile, Ou Traité de L'Éducation,* was published in 1763 in novel form as a plea for the right of children to be children. Rousseau based his theory on the belief that each child is born with his/her own destiny that will unfold in a specific order which is predestined. Each stage of the child's development is different. *Émile* has five parts corresponding to the developmental stages of the child. Rousseau believed that childhood was a special time and education should respond to the needs of each child. Rousseau suggested that we study the child for clues to his or her nature and needs and base education on this information (Duggan, 1936). Child study was unheard of in the eighteenth century. Rousseau also built his system on respect for childhood, emphasizing that children cannot master ideas that they are not ready to learn. Comenius suggested the idea of readiness, but Rousseau clearly stated—children should be allowed to wait for formal education until their physical and emotional development were ready.

Duggan (1936) believes that "the *Émile* was by necessity primarily destructive, and it performed a great service in clearing the ground of much educational rubbish preparatory to laying a new foundation. It is so full of suggestiveness concerning the aims, content, and process of education as to be the starting point of a new education." Rousseau's belief that young children needed a special kind of education requiring more freedom and individuality was radical for its time. Braun and Edwards (1972) believe that Rousseau's impact on education was incalculable because "no thinker after Rousseau could escape dealing with the ideas he set awing in a flurry of feelings." His hypothetical ideas were put into practice in a variety of ways by more practical thinkers.

Johann Heinrich Pestalozzi was a teacher who originated the movement to psychologize education, which resulted in great changes in the aims and methods of elementary education. His work initiated formalization of teacher training techniques. Pestalozzi's work took several forms, including experimentation in industrial education for orphans and the discovery that Rousseau's ideas needed modification. He found that the environment most natural for a child was a home with strict discipline tempered with love. Pestalozzi also wrote about education and social reform. *Leonard and Gertrude* and *How Gertrude Educates Her Children* were written as novels and provided the reader with Pestalozzi's theories of reform.

Pestalozzi put his ideas into practice in three schools for war orphans at which sense impressions gained through work helped children develop ideas. He believed that the hands got the sense impressions which would develop ideas and would in turn develop habits to help form the children's character. At the Stanz, Burgdorf, and Yverdon schools children learned through object lessons proceeding from the simple to the complex and working in an atmosphere of love and kindness each at his/her own pace. This approach replaced memorization and recitation with oral teaching, experience with familiar objects, music, art, spelling, geography, arithmetic, and oral language activities to humanize education. Pestalozzi's actions were his educational doctrine far more than his writings. He believed that educational reform could not take place unless each child was allowed to develop his/her abilities to the fullest and new methods and materials were used. It was in this way, Duggan (1936) believes, that Pestalozzi made his greatest contribution to educational reform.

Scholars and statesmen from Europe and America visited Pestalozzi's schools. His ideas were put into practice in various ways throughout the world. Braun and Edwards (1972) believe that Pestalozzi's connection to the modern kindergarten was his affection and concern for children "and the attempt to protect them as well as instruct them."

Friedrich Wilhelm Froebel was Pestalozzi's most influential student. According to Braun and Edwards (1972), Froebel was the first to develop early childhood education "as a planned, organized portion of the school system...as an entity in its own right." Froebel is the father of the kindergarten. He used the work of Rousseau and Comenius' School of the Mother's Knee to create a garden rather than a schoolroom in which young children would be free to learn about themselves and the world. Influenced by a desire for German national unity, Froebel made unity a central part of his educational philosophy. He saw hidden meaning in natural objects, believing they would reveal the world to children. His belief that development was unfolding the inborn capacities of the child led Froebel to state that the role of education must be to help the child make what is internal, external. Education must help the child develop personality through motor expression and activity in social situations. The child fosters the unfolding process by creative activity; therefore, the education for young children must encourage creativity through play. The child achieves equilibrium between individuality and the curriculum through play. Music, gestures, creative activity, and language development help children express themselves and create an orderly sense of reality. Froebel created special materials and a new environment for the education of the young child. His education was child centered. Modern early childhood materials are directly related to Froebel's original "Gifts and Occupations" —manipulative materials created specifically for young children.

All the pioneers who created modern early childhood education studied the work of Comenius, Rousseau, Pestalozzi, and Froebel, reshaping the ideas and practices in the context of his or her own times and beliefs. These scholars created the foundation on which others continue to build. The transition to modern early childhood education was not a smooth one. It was filled with problems and battles.

A debate within the International Kindergarten Union in the early 1900s led to reforms that shaped the modern kindergarten. The fight between those who advocated strict adherence to Froebelian methods and materials and those who sought reforms based on child study information and Dewey's philosophy split the Union and led to the evolution of modern early childhood education. This new field, based on scientific study of the nature and needs of young children drawn from the work of Dewey, Gesell, Piaget, Montessori, and many other pioneers, reshaped the world's vision of education. As we look forward to the next century we must also look back to our origins to understand the foundation of the field on which new pioneers will build their ideas.

The readers of this volume will be able to locate the primary works of each pioneer, trace the history of early childhood education, and, perhaps, be inspired to find new solutions to existing problems.

BIBLIOGRAPHY

Bayles, Ernest E., and Bruce L. Hood. *Growth of American Educational Thought and Practice.* New York: Harper & Row, 1966.

Braun, Samuel J., and Esther P. Edwards. *History and Theory of Early Childhood Education.* Worthington, Ohio: Charles Jones, 1972.

Curtis, S. J., and E. A. Boultwood. *A Short History of Educational Ideas.* London: University Tutorial Press, 1961.

deGrumps, Baron Rodger. *Pestalozzi: His Life and Work.* Trans. J. Russell. New York: Appleton, 1890.

Duggan, Stephen. *A Student's Textbook in the History of Education.* New York: Appleton-Century, 1936.

Foxley, B. *Émile by Jean-Jacques Rousseau.* New York: Dutton, 1911.

Froebel, Friedrick. *The Education of Man.* Trans. William N. Hailmann. New York: Appleton, 1889.

Keating, M. W. *The Great Didactic of Johann Amos Comenius.* London: A & C Black, 1921.

Pounds, Ralph. *The Development of Education in Western Culture.* New York: Appleton-Century-Crofts, 1968.

Rudolph, Margurita, and Dorothy Cohen. *Kindergarten: A Year of Learning.* New York: Appleton-Century-Crofts, 1964.

Thut, I.N. *The Story of Education: Philosophical and Historical Foundations.* New York: McGraw-Hill, 1957.

Weber, Evelyn. *The Kindergarten: Its Encounter with Educational Thought in America.* New York: Teachers College Press, 1969.

Weber, Evelyn. *Ideas Influencing Early Childhood Education: A Theoretical Analysis.* New York: Teachers College Press, 1984.

SUGGESTED READINGS

Aries, Philippe. *Centuries of Childhood.* New York: Vintage, 1962.

Frost, Ilse. *The School for Children from Two to Eight.* Boston: Ginn & Co., 1935.

Frost, J. L. *Early Childhood Education Rediscovered.* New York: Holt, Reinhart, and Winston, 1968.

Lambert, Hazel. *Early Childhood Education.* Boston: Allyn & Bacon, 1960.

N.S.S.E. *Forty-Sixth Yearbook: Early Childhood Education.* Chicago: University of Chicago Press, 1947.

Johann Amos Comenius (1592-1670)

A Moravian bishop who believed in social reform through education, Comenius developed a system of education from infancy to the university.

Comenius believed in a universal education with a step-by-step plan of sequentially graded instruction based on learning from real objects. He wrote *The Great Didactic*, a guide suggesting education be divided into age levels, that nothing be taught before a child was ready to understand the concepts, and that education should begin in early childhood to build a basis for later learning. He suggested a teaching method which followed the child's developmental pattern using the five senses and advised that play, games, physical activity, music, and fairy tales should be used to teach children until age 6. Young children from birth to age 6 should be taught at home where they would experience real objects and develop their senses to distinguish between objects. These early experiences with the real world plant the seeds of knowledge which will grow with later experiences. *Orbus Pictus*, the first picture book was introduced by Comenius to reinforce the recognition of everyday objects, develop language skills, and help children learn to use books. He believed that ideas were innate and required first-hand experiences for them to unfold and suggested that six-year old children attend a vernacular school to learn religion, singing, morals, mechanical arts, reading, writing, and mathematics. One of his most important contributions was the belief that education for young children should be an active process involving both the mind and the body in things children enjoy doing.

The Great Didactic was ignored until mid-nineteenth-century German educators rediscovered Comenius. His work proved ahead of its time and served as a model for later educational reforms. Many of the principles of education adopted in the nineteenth century were developed in the seventeenth century by Comenius.

PRIMARY SOURCES

1. *Opera Didactica Omnia.* Amsterdam: Aedilus Academiae Scientiarum Bohemoslovenical, 1657. [*The Great Didactic.* Trans. Maurice W. Keatinge. 2 volumes. London: A. & C. Black, Ltd., 1921-1923. *Didactica Magna.* Trans. Wilhelm Altemoller. Paderborn, Prussia: Ferdinand Schonigh, 1905.] Comenius' philosophy of education containing thirty-three chapters discussing the aim, purpose, organization, content, methods of teaching, discipline, and textbooks to be used. It contains everything necessary to develop a modern system of education including a psychology of human nature, a discussion of the connection between methods and the laws of human growth, and a discussion of the role of education in society.

SECONDARY SOURCES

2. Braun, Samuel and Esther Edwards. *History and Theory of Early Childhood Education.* Worthington, Ohio: Charles Jones, 1972, pp. 30-33. Discusses and analyzes the work of Comenius with a reprint of a brief portion of the *Didactica Magna.*

3. Duggan, Stephen. *A Student's Textbook in the History of Education.* New York: Appleton-Century, 1936, pp. 171-180. A classic source for educational history before the twentieth century. Discusses the work of Comenius with excerpts from *The Great Didactic* and *Orbis Pictus,* which was the first picture book.

4. Ulich, Robert. *History of Educational Thought.* New York: American Book Co., 1968, pp. 188-199. Discusses Comenius' personality and educational system with comparison to Hegel, Darwin, and Bacon, as well as the theory and application of his work. Provides an extensive useful bibliography of primary and secondary sources.

5. Ulich, Robert. *Three Thousand Years of Educational Wisdom: Selections from Great Documents.* Cambridge: Harvard University Press, 1954; 1982 (revised), pp. 339-346. A brief discussion of the life and work of Comenius providing selections from *Didactica Magna* translated by Ulich from a 1905 German translation.

John Dewey (1859-1952)

Dewey's work helped to transform the role of the kindergarten at the turn of the twentieth century and eventually influenced the entire field of early childhood education. Dewey organized the classroom into a community in which children learned in cooperation with each other. He used everyday materials and encouraged child-generated choices about activities and materials. He promoted teacher flexibility, creativity, and responsibility and the introduction of art and music, field trips, and nature studies, to encourage problem solving and independent thinking. The classroom became a model of group living in which the children initiated activities, projects, and play. The teacher became a guide who enabled children to develop social skills by providing opportunities for their practice. Dewey explained that children develop when they are involved with activities that have a purpose. He maintained that firsthand experiences motivate growth in reading, writing, and arithmetic. When exposed to the right materials and role models, children develop skills for later academic learning as well as the flexibility to cope with social and emotional problems.

With Dewey's reinterpretation of the kindergarten emphasis on the social and emotional needs of children, a split developed within the International Kindergarten Union in which one group argued for strict adherence to Froebel's methods and materials and the other for Dewey's reforms. This debate eventually led to a program similar to the modern kindergarten.

No other educational philosopher/practitioner has had more influence on early childhood education than John Dewey. His work, replicated by his students and added to by other philosophers, helped shape practice and theory as we know it today.

PRIMARY SOURCES

6. "Results of Child-Study Applied to Education." *Transactions of the Illinois Society for Child Study,* 1 (January 1895): 18-19. In "The Theory of the Chicago Experiment" (Appendix II), *The Dewey School. The Laboratory School of the University of Chicago 1896-1903,* by Katherine Camp Mayhew and Anna Camp Edwards. New York: D. Appleton-Century, 1936; New York: Atherton Press, 1966, (repr.) pp. 474-476. Presents principles for using the results of child study in education, warning against the misuse of this information. Dewey states that we must remember that a child is a being with his/her own activity and not something to be "educated (or) drawn out."

7. "Plan of Organization of the University Primary School." Privately printed, in 1895. In *John Dewey the Early Works, 1882-1898,* Volume 5: *1895-1898 Early Essays,* ed. Jo Ann Boydston. Carbondale: Southern Illinois University Press, 1972, pp. 223-243. Provides a detailed plan including a two month program of instruction, lists of materials, curriculum and activities, sociological principles, and psychological principles and their educational application for a primary school which affords the opportunity to coordinate social and psychological factors. Theory and practice are presented in detail.

8. "Imagination and Expression." *Kindergarten Magazine* 9 (September 1896): 61-69. Published in part in *Western Drawing Teachers' Association Third Annual Report* (May 1896): 136-138. Discusses drawing as artistic expression and lists ways to help children develop artistic technique.

9. "The Need for a Laboratory School." Statement to President William Rainey Harper (University of Chicago) about 1896. In *John Dewey the Early Works, 1882-1898,* Volume 5: *1895-1898 Early Essays,* ed. Jo Ann Boydston. Carbondale: Southern Illinois University Press, 1972, pp. 433-435. A detailed discussion of the need for graduate schools of pedagogy at American universities. States that the first university to do this will become the recognized leader in the United States. Suggests expanding the existing model school to include additional grades to make it a center for "observation, demonstration and experiment" which would serve as the heart of the graduate program. States that a slight increase in cost would be paid for by an increase in enrollment.

10. "Interest in Relation to Training of the Will." *Second Supplement to the First Yearbook of The National Herbart Society.* Bloomington, Illinois: Pantagraph, 1896, pp. 204-246; rev. and (repr.) Chicago: University of Chicago Press, 1899. Discusses interest and effort in educational tasks presenting methods for developing these in children. Describes kindergarten methods and the teacher's role in channeling a child's interest in the desired direction as the basis for future accomplishments.

11. "A Pedagogical Experiment." *Kindergarten Magazine* 8 (June 1896): 739-741. Describes the primary school at the University of Chicago, which is part of the Pedagogical Department, to provide a connection between theory and practice and a place for experimentation and testing new ideas for the university students. The school operates along three lines: (1) to grade work to the individual needs of each child so that children of various ages can work together; (2) to conduct the school on the belief that the studies of the elementary school will best be mastered if treated as factors in the child's life rather than as studies which need to be mastered; and (3) to make the formal and mechanical subservient to material that has intrinsic worth. Children learn the relatedness of facts and material if they are not presented in isolation. Suggests that this kind of school exists best in cooperation with a university because no one person can specialize in all areas of knowledge and university personnel can work with classroom

teachers. The plan is to expand the school to ages 6 through 12 in a new building which would be impossible without the help of the university.

12. "The University School." Report of an address by Head Professor Dewey before the Pedagogical Club, University of Chicago, Saturday, October 31, 1896; *University Record,* 1 (November 6, 1896): 417-419. In *John Dewey the Early Works, 1882-1898,* Volume 5: *1895-1898 Early Essays,* ed. Jo Ann Boydston. Carbondale: Southern Illinois University Press, 1972, pp. 436-441. Describes the school connected with the university, listing its aims as: (1) to test and critique theory and (2) to add to the knowledge in education in a laboratory, such as one used in the sciences, to create new standards and ideas to lead to gradual changes in conditions. States that the school is a special community in which the very complex environment of society is simplified so that children can participate in activities connected with the home "as a center of protection, shelter, comfort, artistic decoration, and food supply." The activities help children recreate in an orderly way their own experiences to build a solid knowledge foundation based on the child's relation to his/her social environment. Describes the method of integrating content into activities. States that the school is an attempt to study the organization of the curriculum and the relation of content to many ways of expression. The organizing principle has been found, but the hypothesis needs careful testing under various conditions. There is no question about the value of careful experimentation along these lines.

13. "Pedagogy as a University Discipline." *University Record,* 1 (September, 18 and 25, 1896): 353-355, 361-363. In *John Dewey the Early Works, 1882-1898,* Volume 5: *1895-1898 Early Essays,* ed. Jo Ann Boydston. Carbondale: Southern Illinois University Press, 1972, pp. 281-289. Makes a distinction between Normal School teacher training for classroom teachers and a higher level of education needed for administrators and professors of pedagogy. States that there is a need for this advanced training in the form of graduate study at American universities because the field needs direction and systematization from expert sources. Universities are the best places to provide leadership, research in methods and curriculum at all levels, and a theoretical base for education. Provides numerous reasons to justify these ideas concluding that pedagogy falls within "the realm of scientific method and is subject to the intellectual application of law" and that we must be aware of "the importance of education and the extent to which it touches human life."

14. "The Kindergarten and Child-Study." *National Education Association Journal of Proceedings and Addresses* (1897), 585-586. States that child study has grown out of educational and social forces that have been at work for a long time and is "a force to be reckoned with." It represents the attempt to state experience in terms of the individual rather than the whole class and to adopt training to individual needs. The kindergarten provides special opportunities to study children under favorable conditions. Lists three

directions for kindergarten child study and concludes that the study of children is important in the kindergarten because it enables the teacher to translate theory into practice for the good of each child. Translating psychology into kindergarten practice means making it more vital and more personal.

15. "Letter and Statement on Organization of Working a Department of Pedagogy, January, 1897." In *John Dewey the Early Works, 1882-1898*, Volume 5: *1895-1898, Early Essays*, ed. Jo Ann Boydston. Carbondale: Southern Illinois University Press, 1972, pp. 442-447. A letter to University of Chicago President William Rainey Harper describing a fully equipped Department of Pedagogy including excerpts from "Pedagogy as a University Discipline" (see no. 13), highlighting "the various lines of work which are naturally included"—educational sociology, educational psychology, general pedagogy, educational history, and a discussion of manual training. States that there have been applications from teachers who can study at the university and become teaching assistants at the university School.

16. "The Interpretation Side of Child-Study." *Transactions of the Illinois Society for Child Study*, 2 (July 1897): 17-27. In *John Dewey, the Early Works, 1882-1898*, Volume 5: *1895-1988, Early Essays*, ed. Jo Ann Boydston. Carbondale: Southern Illinois University Press, 1972, pp. 211-221. Discusses the sources of interest in child study asking: "How are we to interpret this new interest and this new kind of interest in the child? Where did it come from? What is it for? What may we expect from it?" Identifies and describes three sources or movements in the development of interest in the child: political, aesthetic, and scientific. Concludes that science provides a basis for knowledge about children. Children must be educated for the demands of a complex society and only by studying what the child needs, how he/she must master these needs, what helps and what hinders development can education help. Only science can respond to the demands and solve the problems created by the emotional idealistic interests and political interests.

17. "The Primary-Education Fetich." *Forum*, 25 (May 1898): 315-328. In *Education Today*, ed. Joseph Ratnes. New York: G.P. Putnam's Sons, 1940, pp. 18-35. States that there is a need to reorganize the curriculum in the primary grades to include other areas of interest such as science, history, and the arts instead of overemphasizing reading, writing, and linguistic work. The language arts furnish discipline and the other subjects provide interest for pupils. There is a need to reconcile the subjects of discipline and order in the curriculum with those that appeal to individual needs and abilities to create school reform so that society can clearly see its needs and properly meet them through education.

18. "Principles of Mental Development as Illustrated in Early Infancy." *Transactions of the Illinois Society for Child Study*, 4 (1899): 65-83. Presents an outline of child development from birth, describing characteristics of each stage. Concludes with a list of principles which help explain development.

19. "Play and Imagination in Relation to Early Education." Presented at the School of Psychology, sponsored by the Chicago Kindergarten College, in April 1899. In *Kindergarten Magazine* 2 (1899): 636-640; abstracted in *School Journal,* 58 (1899): 589. States that: (1) the essence of play is growth or an expression of the child's attitude, images, or disposition. Play cannot be taught. Adults can offer direction or suggestions, but unless the child makes the stimuli his/her own by acting on them, the child is only going through motions which are meaningless; (2) it is best to avoid the separation of work and play because to the child play is business; and (3) it is necessary to provide opportunities and materials of positive value so that children move gradually and naturally from play into definite study. Imagination is the inner or mental side of play and is measured by the imagery which finds expression in it. The imagination must have an outlet to help the child build what is reality for him/her. This should result in doing something that helps the child go beyond the imperfect image to correct it. Everyday activities found in the home provide the media for developing the imagination. School subjects can offer ways of developing the cultural imagination as much as games, stories, and Froebel's gifts can. After the presentation there is a discussion and a response by William Torrey Harris who states that it is important "to get into Froebel's spirit" to carry play into purposeful activity.

20. *The School and Society.* Chicago: University of Chicago Press, 1899; 1900 (repr.); 1915 (rev.ed.) The first three chapters are lectures presented to parents in 1899. The rest of the book has material about the University of Chicago elementary school. Chapter 6, "Froebel's Educational Principles" describes the application of Friedrich Froebel's ideas to the practices at the Laboratory School, explaining that there is no kindergarten because Froebel's ideas are used with all the children. Explains that modifications were necessary in activities, but "in spite of the apparently radical character they are true to the spirit of Froebel." Chapter 7, "The Psychology of Occupations," describes activities that parallel social life, such as shop work, cooking, sewing, woodworking, and textile work and how they are used in the university school. Chapter 8, "The Development of Attention," describes attempts to connect kindergarten and primary school work, and providing examples of how children become absorbed in their work and develop reflective attention (the ability of children to connect the means to a remote end and, with increased ability, to think of the end as something to be discovered; children are then able to control actions to help in inquiry and to find a solution). States that classroom activities should include "self-putting of problems and solutions" rather than ready made materials.

21. "The Situation as Regards the Course of Study." *National Education Association Journal of Proceedings and Addresses* (1901): 332-348. An address presented before the Department of Superintendence of the NEA in Chicago, February 28, 1901; *Educational Review,* 22 (June 1901) 26-49; (repr.)

School Journal, 62 (April 20 and 27, 1901; May 4, 1901): 421-423, 445-446, 454, 469-471; (repr.) Quotations and comments in *Kindergarten Magazine,* 13 (June 1901): 574-577. (repr.) Discusses the importance of reforming the elementary school curriculum based on "a coherent philosophy of experience and a philosophy of the relation of school studies to that experience" Describes the problems related to curriculum reform, such as reports of inadequately prepared students. Concludes that much has been done, but more is needed. Sounds very contemporary.

22. "The Child and the Curriculum." *University of Chicago Contributions to Education,* No. 5. Chicago: University of Chicago Press, 1902; (repr.) with *The School and Society,* with an introduction by Leonard Carmichael. Chicago: University of Chicago Press, 1956. Describes how the teacher and students should deal with the content of curriculum, stating there are three dimensions of every subject: (1) the concern of the expert who wants to do research; (2) the concern of the elementary school teacher who is interested in the subject as "representing a given stage...of development of experience" and must be able to present the material as a personal experience; and (3) the concern of the child is how the subject is related to his/her interests, problems, and progress. The teacher of young children should not stress the academic aspects of the subject matter, but use it to "enliven the interest and activity of students." The teacher should present the subject matter so that students can made immediate and personal use of it and avoid focusing on the technical and abstract aspects. Presents a complete picture of methodology.

23. "Activity, Logical Theory and Educational Implications of." *A Cyclopedia of Education,* ed. Paul Monroe. Vol. 1. New York: Macmillan, 1911, pp. 33-34. Discusses activity in education stating that self-activity "is losing its purely philosophical meaning and is becoming associated with all types of directed action in which purpose, choice, and reflection of the individual takes a part." Froebel's concept of kindergarten was based on this idea after he rediscovered Plato's idea of the importance of play and occupation activity in education. The introduction of cooking, art, woodworking, and sewing into the curriculum shows that these activities serve important cognitive and moral purposes. The use of laboratory work in the sciences is also an example of this important principle in education.

24. "Reasoning in Early Childhood." Paper presented before the Department of Kindergarten Education, Teachers College Alumni Conference, February 21, 1913; *Teachers College Record* 15 (January 1914): 9-15. Describes the reasoning process in the young child with emphasis on the implications for activities at the kindergarten age level.

25. and Evelyn Dewey. *Schools of Tomorrow.* New York: E.P. Dutton, 1915, 1943, 1962; London; J.M. Dent, 1915, [*Las Escuelas Di Mañana* Trans. Lorenzo Luzuriaga. Madrid: Hernsndo, 1918; *Shkoli Budushchigo* Trans. R. Landsberg. Moscow: Robotnik Prosveshcheneya, 1922; *Les Écoles*

De Demain Trans. R. Duthill. Paris: Ernest Flammarion, 1931.] A description of schools in Georgia, New York, Chicago, Indianapolis, Illinois, and Indiana that put the theories of Jean-Jacques Rousseau, Frederich Froebel, Johann Pestalozzi, Maria Montessori, and other philosophers into practice. Dewey and his daughter Evelyn reported on the experimental schools that were ahead of their time using open classroom and activity-based techniques. The theorists are referred to in the description of each school. Dewey stated that the book was not intended as a textbook to develop theories of education or to review programs or ideas of well-known educators or as a guide to teachers, but to show what really happens when schools put into practice, "each in its own way, some of the theories that have been pointed out to be the best and the soundest." Shows the contrast between progressive education and conventional education in place in the early twentieth century. The book shows clearly that Dewey knew how difficult it would be to change educational practice.

26. *Democracy and Education: An Introduction to the Philosophy of Education.* New York: Macmillan, 1916. In Chapter 12, "Thinking in Education," the importance of firsthand experience at every age level is described. Children need to try to do something with materials on their own, they do not need predigested secondhand ideas. Children must use trial and error the way scientists do; therefore, content should be taught with every day experiences that happen outside of school and that will motivate children to develop thinking skills. In Chapter 15, "Play and Work in the Curriculum," Dewey states that play and work have intellectual and social value and must be part of the curriculum. The school should not overemphasize teacher control of activities. While the Froebelian kindergarten feared raw materials, Dewey believed that only when children work with raw materials in a purposeful way will they "gain the intelligence embodied in the finished material." Children do not need predigested ideas, but need to discover the truth within situations and solve problems themselves to discover what things can do and the learning that results from discovering ideas for one's self.

27. "The Dewey School Statements: General History; Experimental Activities, Developing Skills in Communication and Expression; Teachers and School Organization; and Evaluation of Principles and Practices." In *The Dewey School: The Laboratory School of the University of Chicago, 1896-1903,* by Katherine Camp Mayhew and Anna Camp Edwards. New York: D. Appleton-Century, 1936; New York: Atherton Press, 1966, (repr.) pp. 5-7, 361-362, 365-367, 370-372, 414-415, 417, 431-432. Original statements and comments written by Dewey for each section provide support for the Mayhew and Edwards commentary.

28. "The Theory of the Chicago Experiment. Appendix II." In *The Dewey School: The Laboratory School of the University of Chicago, 1896-1904,* by Katherine Camp Mayhew and Anna Camp Edwards. New York: D.

Appleton-Century, 1936; New York: Atherton, 1966, (repr.) pp. 463-477. Discusses the gap between educational theory and practice, describing the need for and use of the Laboratory School, referring to "Plan of Organization" (see no. 7); "Pedagogy as a University Discipline" (see no. 13); "The Interpretation Side of Child-Study" (see no. 16); and *Democracy and Education* (see #27) to support his statements.

29. *Experience and Education.* New York: Macmillan, 1938, The Kappa Delta Pi lecture, delivered at Atlantic City, New Jersey, March 1, 1938. Explains how experience should be the power in education and life and relates the two ideas Dewey thought were the most basic in a theory of experience—interaction and continuity. States that there must be a connection between education and personal experience because the most important characteristic of experience is its interactive nature. Also, one cannot ignore the situation or the status of the learner for effective education. This is Dewey's most concise statement of his ideas about the problems, needs, and potential of education. It restates ideas and urges teachers to look for the deeper and bigger issues in education and not to look to "isms" to solve problems. States that American education should respect all types of experience and offer a true learning situation.

SECONDARY SOURCES

30. Baker, Edna Dean. "The Kindergarten in Illinois." Presented at the Cincinnati Convention of the Association for Childhood Education, April 1923, 1938. In *History of the Kindergarten Movement in the Mid-Western States and in New York,* eds. Lucy Wheelock, Caroline D. Aborn, and Sarah A. Marble. Washington, D.C.: Association for Childhood Education, 1938, pp. 18-23. Describes the kindergarten in Illinois, attributes the experimental school at the University of Chicago directed by Professor Dewey as having "demonstrated the influence of the kindergarten principles upon primary methods and was vital in arousing interest in child study and in the principles and practices of the kindergarten." Describes the history of the Kindergarten Department at the University of Chicago.

31. Brickman, William and Stanley Lehrer, eds. *John Dewey: Master Educator.* New York: Society for the Advancement of Education, 1959, 1961. A 100th birthday tribute to Dewey which includes papers by William Heard Kilpatrick, Maxine Green, Franklin Parker, Junius I. Meriam, and others. Topics include Dewey's philosophy, his role at the University of Chicago, historical perspective and Dewey as a teacher. An outline of Dewey's life and work, a list of his letters, and a list of related writings are included.

32. Cavallo, Dominick. "From Perfection to Habit: Moral Training in the American Kindergarten, 1860-1920." *History of Education Quarterly,* 16 (Summer 1976): 147-161. Describes the struggle between the Froebelians and the Progressives for control of the kindergarten curriculum and highlights

the social importance and educational consequence of the struggle. Describes the Progressive critique of the Froebelian kindergarten, 1890-1920, providing information on Dewey's Laboratory School in Chicago. Concludes with a discussion of the moral training idea of the Progressives and its impact on kindergarten practice.

33. Chase, Francis. S. "The Chicago Laboratory School: Retrospect and Prospect." *UCLA Educator* 21 (Winter 1980): 38-44. Presents a history of the University of Chicago Laboratory School (1894-1904), stating that Dewey's theory was the foundation for the curriculum and activities. Describes the four schools that existed in the 1970s at the university and compares the internal problems faced by the turn of the century school and the schools of the 1970s review the contributions of theory to practice, and presents scenarios for the future of the school.

34. Clippinger, Geneva M. "A Visit to the Sub-Primary Class of Dr. Dewey's School." *Kindergarten Review* 11 (March 1901): 424-426. Describes the activities and the children's behavior, stating that everyone worked independently and spontaneously and during lunchtime the children were completely responsible for the preparation of food, serving, and washing up. Provided a view of daily routines.

35. Cremin, Lawrence A. *The Transformation of the School. Progressivism in American Education, 1876-1957.* New York: Knopf, 1962, pp. 99-142. Describes Dewey's philosophy, his interest in psychology, the work at the University of Chicago Laboratory School, and his aims of education, referring to Dewey's writings to illustrate points. Provides details about the Laboratory School and states that Dewey believed that "the continuing quest for further improvement (was)…the central task of the science of education."

36. Cremin, Lawrence A. *American Education. The Metropolitan Experience 1876-1980.* New York: Harper & Row, 1988, pp. 164-196. A comprehensive analysis of Dewey's influence on American education. Provides extensive biographical notes.

37. Cross, Ermine. "The Work of the Chicago Free Kindergarten Association Amour Institute." *Kindergarten Magazine* 10 (April 1898): 509-515. Describes the contributions of Dewey and others to the teacher training program under the direction of Anna E. Bryan, who worked closely with Dewey to develop the sub-primary program at the Chicago University Laboratory School.

38. Curti, Merle. *The Social Ideas of American Educators with a New Chapter on the Last Twenty-five Years.* New Jersey: Littlefield, Adams & Co., 1965, pp. 499-541. An analysis of Dewey's social ideas and an evaluation of his criticisms of social and educational ideas. Provides extensive footnotes, but an inadequate bibliography.

39. DePencier, Ida B. *The History of the Laboratory School: The University of Chicago, 1896-1965.* Chicago: Quadrangle, 1967. Presents a history of

the University of Chicago Laboratory School from its founding in 1896 by Dewey, cites the influences of Johann Pestalozzi and Friedrich Froebel on Dewey's ideas, and traces in detail the growth of the school through 1965. There is a detailed discussion of the kindergarten program throughout the history of the school and an analysis of Dewey's it.

40. Dykhuizen, George. *The Life and Mind of John Dewey.* Carbondale: Southern Illinois University Press, 1973. A detailed biography with photographs and chapter notes.

41. Eisele, Chris. "The Dewey School: A Record of Success and A Reality of Failure." *Journal of the Midwestern History of Education Society* 12 (1984): 29-39. Part I describes the way the University of Chicago Laboratory School has been historically important in history of education textbooks. Part II states that Dewey did not complete his experiment even though he set up a framework for the study and improvement of education. Dewey left Chicago in 1904 when the experiment was in its early stages. Presents extensive evidence for both ideas. Concludes that: historians have not done a thorough examination of the school and that Progressive education failed because there was no convincing history of the education of Progressive teachers.

42. Green, Maxine. "Dewey and American Education 1894-1920." *School and Society* 87 (October 10, 1959): 259, 381-386. Asks the questions What were the effects of Dewey's work at the time it was done? What was the actual response to John Dewey during his active and productive years? Answers them by examining Dewey's influence on educational theory, the effects of his writing, teaching, and example on educational practice. Provides an in-depth discussion of Dewey's writing, the Laboratory School, and material about Dewey. Concludes that it took more than twenty years for educators to free themselves from their traditions to "discover what Dewey actually said" about a philosophy of experience, the scientific method, and the social job of the schools.

43. Hendley, Brian Patrick. *Dewey, Russell, Whitehead: Philosophers as Educators.* Carbondale: Southern Illinois University Press, 1986, pp. 14-42. States that philosophers of education should stop defining terms and analyzing ideas and go back to building theories of education as Dewey did. Provides a detailed account of the University of Chicago Laboratory School as an example of theory testing. Describes the Dewey School, the theory behind it, some recent criticism of Dewey's educational theory, and remarks on theory and practice in education. Provides an extensive bibliography of primary and secondary sources.

44. Kowalski, Theodore J, John A. Glober, and Damon Krug. "The Role of the Laboratory School on Providing a Research Base for Teacher Education," *Contemporary Education* 60, no. 1 (Fall 1988): 19-22. Provides a brief history of Laboratory School research with a focus on the Dewey School; reviews the results of two surveys done in the 1980s to evaluate the pro-

ductivity of modern laboratory schools; states reasons for low levels of research productivity; and concludes with recommendations for changing Laboratory Schools into laboratories for the discovery of new knowledge about teaching and learning.

45. Lazerson, Marvin. "The Historical Antecedents of Early Childhood Education." In *Early Childhood Education. The Seventy-first Yearbook of the National Society for the Study of Education Part II,* ed. Ira Gordon. Chicago: University of Chicago Press, 1972, pp. 33-54. States that Dewey was the most influential person in the Progressive kindergarten reform movement because he rejected the excessive order of the Froebelians in favor of more individual choice among activities, basing activities on daily living at home and in the community, and less teacher direction. Dewey's most important contribution was the idea that problem solving and socialization should be the basis for the activities of young children who need to solve real problems, make plans, and complete the tasks they plan.

46. Mayhew, Katherine Camp and Anna Camp Edwards. *The Dewey School: The Laboratory School of the University of Chicago 1896-1903.* New York: D. Appleton-Century, 1936; New York: Atherton, 1966. (repr.) A comprehensive history of the University of Chicago Laboratory School by two of its original teachers. Provides a detailed record of the aims, methods, philosophy, activities, curriculum, personnel, and involvement of parents and children, as well as an evaluation of the principles and practices of the school. Includes an introduction by Dewey, an evaluation Dewey's principles of education, and the theory of the Chicago Experiment, which includes material written by Dewey. This is a firsthand account of the application of Dewey's theory of education to classroom practice.

47. McCaul, Robert L. "Dewey's Chicago." *School Review* 67, no. 2 (Summer 1959): 258-280. Describes the social, political, and intellectual atmosphere in Chicago and at the University of Chicago at the turn of the twentieth century that provided Dewey with the freedom and support to develop his educational and philosophical ideas. Provides extensive footnotes.

48. McCaul, Robert L. "Dewey and the University of Chicago." *School and Society,* Part I, March 25, 1961, 152-157; Part II, April 8, 1961, 179-183: Part III, April 22, 1961, 202-206; also in *John Dewey: Master Educator,* eds. William Brickman and Stanley Lehrer. New York: Society for the Advancement of Education, 1961, pp. 31-74. Presents what McCaul calls a "circumstantial account" of Dewey's resignation from the University of Chicago in 1904 with many quotations from documents presenting evidence in the words of Dewey and President William Rainey Harper. The three articles cover the following time periods: Part I, July 1894–March 1902; Part II, April 1902–May 1903; and Part III, September 1903–June 1904. Each article describes the situation at the university, the Laboratory School, and the events during each time period. Provides extensive foot-

notes using letters and other archival material.

49. McCluskey, Neil Gerard. *Public Schools and Moral Education. The Influence of Horace Mann, William Torrey Harris, and John Dewey.* Part 4. New York: Columbia University Press, 1958. Provides biographical information and an analysis of Dewey's contributions to philosophy and education. States that "John Dewey, who attempted to fuse the imperatives of science and nature, democracy and humanity has in some measure touched every stone in the modern American educational structure." William Kilpatrick is quoted as saying that Dewey did what no previous philosopher after Johann Pestalozzi could do, he developed "an adequate theory for a thorough going, democratic science respecting education." Provides a chronological bibliography of primary sources and a shorter bibliography of secondary sources.

50. "Reports of Lectures by John Dewey, before the Federation for Child Study," by Jenny B. Merrill. I. "Lecture on Rousseau, Pestalozzi, Froebel, and Montessori," *Kindergarten-Primary Magazine,* 26 (March 1914): 186; II. "Lecture on Social Motives in School Life," *Kindergarten-Primary Magazine,* 26 (April 1914): 215; III. "Lecture on Pestalozzi," *Kindergarten-Primary Magazine,* 26 (May 1914): 251; IV. "A Comparison of Herbart and Froebel," *Kindergarten-Primary Magazine,* 26 (May 1914): 255-256. Presents a summary of Dewey's series of lectures at the Ethical Cultural Society in New York, January 13 through February 10, 1914. I. Explains the educational theories of each philosopher and their relation to 20th-century educational practices. II. Discusses the social aspect of classroom living and how to adapt the curriculum and activities to provide for social living. III. Discusses Johann Pestalozzi's philosophy in detail, relating his ideas to classroom activities in early childhood education. IV. A comparison of the work of Friedrich Froebel and Johann Friedrich Herbart in relation to kindergarten classroom practice. States that the chief objection to prevalent kindergarten ideas is that they educate through artificial symbols rather than through social life. Kindergartens generally do not study children and do not experiment enough. Herbart questioned formal discipline and used Pestalozzi's ideas. Froebel and Herbart believed in a technical system of education.

51. Sarason, Seymour B. *The Culture of the School and the Problem of Change.* Boston: Allyn & Bacon, 1971, pp. 195-211. Based on the Mayhew and Edwards 1936 book (see no. 47), it describes the University of Chicago Laboratory (or Dewey) School as an alternative to the schools of that time. States that the Mayhew and Edwards book is the most comprehensive discussion of a school ever written presenting not only Dewey's ideas, but their relation to practice with details of classroom activities. Even though Mayhew and Edwards were part of the experiment and may present a biased view, they are candid about the problems, mistakes, and failures they experienced. Sarason focuses on the principal, the teacher, and the

realization of theory into classroom method. Sarason concludes that his aim was to describe the culture of the Dewey School as one very different from what we have today to emphasize that alternatives are available. The Dewey School was not organized the way model schools are today, from an idea of what children were like as a group or as individuals, but from the idea that school was truly a social place in which the thinking and contributions of all members of the culture were entwined and each person had a legitimate stake and function in deciding what the school would be like.

52. Scates, Georgia P. "The Sub-Primary (Kindergarten) Department." *The Elementary School Record* 1 (June 1900): 129-142. Describes the daily schedule and activities of the program stating that they are different from Froebelian kindergartens. Observes children using a variety of objects to make playhouse furniture.

53. Shapiro, Michael Steven. *Child's Garden. The Kindergarten Movement from Froebel to Dewey.* University Park: The Pennsylvania State University Press, 1983, pp. 151-191. Describes Dewey's Chicago Laboratory School and his influence on the progressive kindergarten reform movement. Provides extensive bibliography notes.

54. Ulich, Robert. *History of Educational Thought.* New York: American Book Co., 1968, pp. 315-336. An analysis of Dewey's educational program and the relation of that program to his philosophical program; a critique of his general philosophy; and a critique of his educational philosophy. Lengthy bibliography of primary and secondary sources.

55. Weber, Evelyn. *Ideas Influencing Early Childhood Education. A Theoretical Analysis.* New York: Teachers College Press, 1984, pp. 86-103. Discusses Dewey's philosophy and contributions to early childhood education with an analysis of the Laboratory School; his influence on Alice Temple and the Progressive Kindergarten Reform Movement; his rejection of Friedrich Froebel's curriculum; Dewey's instrumentalism, including his theory of learning by doing, *Democracy and Education,* including the appeal of his philosophy to the kindergarten leaders; and Dewey's legacy to early childhood education. States that Dewey had faith in the common school and his philosophy had a long view "without quick payoffs." Extensive endnotes of primary and secondary sources. Provides background for a more in-depth study of Dewey's work.

56. Westbrook, Robert B. *John Dewey and American Democracy.* Ithaca: Cornell University Press, 1991. A biography that analyzes the development of Dewey's philosophy and his view of democracy. Extensive bibliographic notes.

57. Wheelock, Lucy and Barbara Greenwood, eds. *History of the Kindergarten Movement in the Western States, Hawaii and Alaska.* Presented at the 47th Annual Convention of the Association for Childhood Education, Milwaukee, Wisconsin, 1940. Washington, D.C.: Association for Childhood

Education, 1940, pp. 63-67. Describes the founding of the Henry and Dorothy Castle Memorial Free Kindergarten in Honolulu in 1900 with a teacher trained by Dewey in Chicago, because Dewey's ideas about education as a form of community life incorporating home and community activities into the curriculum suited the needs of the school's diverse population. In 1922 Grade 1 was added; in 1923 three-year-olds were enrolled; and in 1927 a nursery school was added.

58. Wirth, Arthur G. "The Psychological Theory for Experimentation in Education at John Dewey's Laboratory School, The University of Chicago, 1896-1904." *Educational Theory* 16 (1966): 271-280. Examines the theoretical rational that formed the basis for the Laboratory School, stating that Dewey believed that teaching could only become a profession when its members became students of subject matter and mind activity. The university had the responsibility of creating, through research, a theory and philosophy of education that would be its foundation. This work could only be done in a Laboratory School which would serve the same purpose as a science laboratory. Describes the process of theory development and testing.

59. Wirth, Arthur G. *John Dewey as Educator. His Design for Work in Education (1894-1904).* New York: John Wiley & Sons, 1966; New York: Robert E. Krieger, 1979.(repr.) Part I discusses the philosophical and psychological theories from which Dewey's educational ideas developed. Part II describes the curriculum and methodology in the Laboratory School, with a post-script that tries to show the bridge between Dewey's theory and practice while he was still a practicing educator.

60. Wood, Jacalyn. "The Dewey School Revisited." *Childhood Education* 58 (November-December 1981): 99-101. Examines Dewey's Chicago experiment to gain insight into curriculum areas and instructional methods which can be applied to "back to basics" teaching. Describes the social occupations curriculum, cooperative efforts, and principles of growth. Concludes with the chapter "Past, Present and Future," which describes the Chicago Laboratory School in the 1980s stating that "educators do not need to start from scratch" but can use Dewey's ideas as the foundation for instruction in the basics.

Ella Victoria Dobbs (1866-1952)

A commitment to the wider use of manual arts in the kindergarten led Dobbs to work for more continuity of curriculum in the elementary school.

Dobbs made many other contributions to education. She was a founding member and president (1915-1925) of the National Council of Primary Education; professor and department chairperson in the Department of Applied Arts which she created at the University of Missouri, and she developed a complete curriculum for handwork in the elementary school as a separate division of applied arts. She was a founding member of Pi Lambda Theta (president, 1921-1925), Columbia Missouri's first parent-teachers group, the Equal Suffrage Association, and a branch of the League of Women Voters; and served as president of the Missouri State Teachers Association (1925). In 1923 Pi Lambda Theta initiated the Ella Victoria Dobbs scholarship for advanced study in education. The Women's Centennial Congress in 1940 honored her as one of 100 women who succeeded in careers not open to women in 1840; and she was honored by Missouri as a leader in achieving women's suffrage and by the Association for Childhood Education as a leader in early childhood education. In addition, she was an accomplished author and lecturer.

Dobbs believed that teachers should experiment to improve methods and use applied arts projects to teach content across the curriculum. She worked to help teachers become involved, interested, and committed to community and educational activities.

PRIMARY SOURCES

61. *Primary Handwork.* New York. Macmillan, 1914. Describes artwork projects for young children to be used with various curriculum areas.

62. *Illustrative Handwork for Elementary School Subjects.* New York: Macmillan, 1917. A comprehensive book for teachers that discusses how to use handwork across the curriculum, detailed directions for using a variety of materials; four types of activities—posters, illustrated books, table representations, and illustrative construction; student textbooks in a variety of subject areas and relates to the projects; and a list of projects. Most relevant today in light of integrated curriculum. Perhaps Dobbs was years ahead of her time?

63. *Our Playhouse.* Chicago: Rand McNally, 1924. Written for second grade children, this book presents a detailed description of how a group of children planned and built a playhouse. Presents a brief discussion for teachers at the end telling how they can use the book with children.

64. and Lucy Gage, Julia L. Hahn. *History of the National Council of Primary Education.* National Council of Primary Education, 1932, typed pamphlet in Archives, Association for Childhood Education International, University of Maryland, McKeldin Library. Describes the founding of the NCPE in February 1915. It was established to encourage activities in the primary school, provide teachers with freedom of choice of teaching methods, and to foster closer cooperation between the kindergarten and the elementary grades. The NCPE merged with the International Kindergarten Union and became part of the Association for Childhood Education in 1931. Includes descriptions of all meetings through 1931, listing topics and speakers. Most of the major figures in early childhood education such as Abigail Adams Eliot, Lucy Gage, Lucy Sprague Mitchell, Colonel Francis Parker, Patty Smith Hill, and Alice Temple presented papers or were speakers at meetings.

65. *First Steps in Weaving.* New York: Macmillan, 1938. A book for beginners providing a complete history of weaving. Quotes a weaver, who said "it isn't so much that you weave as what weaving does to you," to say that this statement "epitomizes what is meant by creative expression as an educational factor."

SECONDARY SOURCES

66. "Columbia Branch of A.A.U.W. Holds Banquet." *Columbia Missourian,* May 20, 1949, p. 3, col. 1. Pictures and describes honorees of the A.A.U.W. as pioneers. Dobbs is honored as the founder of Pi Lambda Theta and Delta Kappa Gamma Honor Societies for educators and for her fifty years in education, twentyseven at the University of Missouri's Department of Industrial Arts.

67. "Ella V. Dobbs Dies in Macon, Mo." *Columbia Missourian,* April 14, 1952, p. 1, col. 7. This obituary discusses Dobbs' work in the arts and her long teaching career. It names the pallbearers and survivors and describes the memorial to be established at the Calvary Episcopal Church.

68. "Ella V. Dobbs Given Office." *Columbia Missourian,* November 15, 1924, p. 1, col. 3. Announces that Dobbs has been elected president of the Missouri State Teachers Association, only the second woman in history of the organization to hold that office. Describes Dobbs' qualifications and lists other officers.

69. "Ella V. Dobbs Speaks on Art: Purpose of Teaching it in School is to Give Appreciation." *Columbia Missourian,* July 6, 1926, p. 2, col. 2. Describes Dobbs' lecture on "Every Day Art for Every Day People," stating that everyone can express him/herself in the language of beauty if art is part of everyone's education. Discusses the importance of art appreciation in education for all ages.

70. "P.T.A. to Honor Miss Ella Dobbs." *Columbia Missourian,* April 26, 1950, p. 1B, col. 1-2. The Columbia P.T.A. honored Dobbs with membership

because of her work in 1911 to establish a Mothers Club. Through Dobbs' efforts, bylaws and a constitution for the Council of Mothers' Clubs and a P.T.A. in Boone County was founded in 1918. Discusses Dobb's work as a professor in industrial arts and her work with local, state, and national educational organizations.

71. "7 Legislative Changes will be Proposed. Ella V. Dobbs Describes Educational Program of State to Women Voters." *Columbia Missourian,* December 16, 1926, p. 1. Dobbs describes the Missouri Educational Program to the League of Women Voters. The seven points for legislative consideration were: (1) Legalization of kindergartens in the state if communities wanted them. States that kindergartens would soon be part of the regular school system instead of a separate school. (2) Establishment of junior colleges; (3) Compulsory attendance law amendment. (4) Minimum salary required for teachers. (5) Provisions to upgrade qualifications for teachers. (6) Reorganization of the office of County Superintendent. (7) Redistricting to create adequate size districts to support elementary schools and a high school.

72. Snyder, Agnes. *Dauntless Women in Childhood Education, 1856-1931,* Washington, D.C.: Association for Childhood Education International, 1972, pp. 283-320. Presents a biography and an analysis of Dobbs work in manual arts at the University of Missouri. Highlights her work with the P.T.A., the League of Women Voters, and community service.

73. Wulfckammer, Verna M. *Ella Victoria Dobbs, A Portrait Biography.* Missouri: George Banta, Phi Lambda Theta, 1961. A complete biography intended as a memorial to Dobbs written by a colleague.

Abigail Adams Eliot (1892-1992)

A student of Margaret McMillan, Eliot helped establish the nursery school movement in America.

Eliot was the founder, with Elizabeth W. Pearson, of the Ruggles Street Nursery School and Training Center and the Nursery Training School of Boston. From 1922-1952 she served as director; in 1952 the Training School became the Eliot-Pearson Department of Child Study at Tufts University. She was a founding member of the National Association of Nursery Education, which became the National Association for the Education of Young Children in 1964; was a member of the National Advisory Committee for the Federal Emergency Relief Administration to establish emergency nursery schools during the Depression; and established the Pacific Oaks College in Pasadena, California, in 1952. Her commitment to parental involvement in education helped parents establish a cooperative, the Cambridge Nursery School. She believed that children are persons, that education should be guidance to develop personalities, and educational programs should be balanced to help children become secure and independent.

Eliot believed that nursery school education was not custodial care, but a genuine educational program. Her work reflected an interest in and a respect for children.

PRIMARY SOURCES

74. "Two Nursery Schools: Nurseries Working on Health, Education, and Family Life." *Child Health Magazine* (March 1924): 97-101. Discusses the work and aims of the Ruggles Street and Cambridge Nursery Schools, which served two different populations. Discusses the value and importance of nursery school education for the future. Describes the equipment, daily routine, contact with the mother, and school objectives. Photographs of the Ruggles Street Schoolyard are included. One school was a private, self-supporting school managed by a committee of parents, and the other, Ruggles Street was organized as a philanthropy and an educational experiment. However, the aim of both schools was the same: to develop the mind and body of preschool children.

75. "Department of Nursery Education. Educating the Parents Through the Nursery School." *Childhood Education* 1, no. 3 (December 1926): 183-189. States that without the active participation of parents the total development of children would not be possible. Describes parent activities at the Cambridge Nursery School and the Ruggles Street Nursery School asking and answering several questions: Parent cooperation—Why? Parent co-

operation—How? Eliot describes how parents cooperate and participate in the school such as conferences on request when parents can ask for a conference with a teacher at anytime; psychological discussions for mothers by mothers, a series of discussions organized and presented by parents for parents; the mother "on duty," a plan whereby a mother can come to help; the casual conference or unplanned informal discussion with a teacher; the visiting mother or an invited observation by a mother; and round-table discussions between a group of parents and teachers on a specific topic. Concludes that the "nursery school reemphasizes the need and the possibility of real cooperation between parents and teachers in the vital work of guiding child development...because at this early age...what the school wishes to accomplish cannot be done by the school alone."

76. "Nursery School Fifty Years Ago." *Childhood Education* 27, no. 4 (April 1972): 209-214. Discusses the nursery school movement in England and the United States; the contributions of John Dewey, Robert Owen, Maria Montessori, and Margaret McMillan; the work of Patty Smith Hill; the founding of Ruggles Street Nursery School and Training Center; the aims of nursery school education; and compares Ruggles Street and the Merrill-Palmer School. Although Arnold Gesell stated in 1924 that the educational ladder did not touch the ground, Eliot concludes that, since the founding of the Ruggles Street and other nursery schools the ladder has reached the ground and "people are working to make its footing even more solid."

SECONDARY SOURCES

77. "Abigail Adams Eliot, 100, Dies: Expert in Nursery School Training." *New York Times,* November 2, 1992, p. D12. This obituary discusses Eliot's training at the Rachel McMillan Training Center in London, the establishment of the Ruggles Street Nursery School, and work in the Roosevelt administration organizing emergency nurseries. Biographical information is given.

78. Gesell, Arnold L. "The Preschool Child as a Health Problem." *American Journal of Nursing* (1923): 1-4. Discusses the health-related problems found in preschool age children.

79. Gesell, Arnold, L. "The Preschool Child: His Social Significance." *The Annals of the American Academy of Political and Social Sciences* 105 (January 1923): 277-280. Selects three outstanding nursery schools: the Merrill-Palmer School in Detroit, a New York school founded by Harriet M. Johnson, and the Ruggles Street Nursery School. Describes the schools as "experimental on a voluntary and pioneer basis." Provides insight into the importance of nursery school education in the development of the child.

80. Gesell, Arnold, L. *The Preschool Child from the Standpoint of Public Hygiene and Education.* Boston: Houghton-Mifflin, 1923. Describes the objectives of the Ruggles Street Nursery school: (1) to create the right envi-

ronment for the child, and (2) to demonstrate the value of physical, mental, and moral care to parents. Eliot's school is one of several discussed.

81. "In Memoriam, Abigail Adams Eliot." *Young Children* 48 (March 1993): 3, 52. Describes Eliot's work with the National Association for Nursery Education, which became the National Association for the Education of Young Children, and her early work in Boston Children's Mission. The article calls Eliot a pioneer and a missionary in the field of early childhood education. A photograph is included.

82. Pearson, Elizabeth Winsor. "The Ruggles Street Nursery School. The Cambridge Nursery School." *Progressive Education* 2, no. 1 (January-March 1925): 19-21. Describes the physical facilities and the programs of the two very different nursery schools. Discusses Eliot's educational background and her leadership at the Ruggles Street Nursery School and Training Center which trained nursery school teachers. Praises both the Ruggles Street and the Cambridge nursery schools for their contributions to their respective communities.

Friedrich Wilhelm Froebel (1782-1852)

Froebel developed a theory and detailed method for educating young children called the kindergarten.

Contributions to education made by Froebel include a belief that learning should be an active process, the inclusion of play as an educational method, and the understanding that childhood is a unique time. He suggested a cooperative social environment rather than a competitive environment and put forth the belief that education was a process of unfolding of abilities. His child-centered curriculum included self-activity, physical activity, music, outdoor activities, and a series of manipulative materials called "Gifts and Occupations," which used the senses, followed a specific sequence, and provided detailed teacher directions. He advocated the training of young women as teachers; the development of songs and finger-plays for home and school; and wrote numerous books including *The Education of Man* and *The Pedagogics of the Kindergarten.*

Froebel attempted to build a new system of education suited to the needs of young children and that would provide materials to help children organize and understand the world. This became a systematic, organized connection between theory and practice on which other pioneers built to create early childhood education.

PRIMARY SOURCES

83. *Padagogik Des Kindergarten.* Berlin: W. Lang, 1862. [*Pedagogics of the Kindergarten.* Trans. Josephine Jarvis, New York: D. Appleton & Co., 1895.] Discussion of the theory of unity, interrelatedness of all educational experiences, the conditions of child development, and the kindergarten program. Describes in precise detail the use of the Gifts by children and the importance of songs, games, and movement.

84. *Mutter Und Kose-Lieder.* Wein und Liepzig: F. Seedel, 1883. ["The Mother Play and Nursery Songs" Trans. Bertha von Marenholtz-Bulow. In *The Kindergarten and Child Culture Papers,* ed. Henry Barnard. Hartford: Office of Barnard's American Journal of Education, 1890, pp. 227-350. *Mottoes and Commentaries of Froebel's Mother Play.* Trans. Henriette R. Eliot. Prose commentaries translated and introduction on Froebel's philosophy by Susan E. Blow. New York: Appleton & Co., 1906.] The poems, pictures, mottoes, fingerplays, and commentaries intended for mothers to use with infants as a child development guide. This material is the basis for part of the modern early childhood curriculum. Used by Froebel as the basis for his lectures to illustrate his theory.

85. *Memschen Erziehung.* Wein und Liepzig: G.A. Lidner, 1883. [*The Educa-tion of Man.* Trans. William N. Hailmann. New York: D. Appleton, 1899.] Statement of Froebel's philosophical creed, the importance of play, and the philosophy on which his theory of early childhood education is based. A better translation of the title would be *People's Education.*
86. *Kindergarten Briefe.* Wien und Liepzig: Hermann Poesche, 1887. [*Letters on the Kindergarten.* Trans. Hermann Poesche, Emilie Michaelis, and H. Keatley Moore. Syracuse: C.W. Bardeen, 1906.] Letters about the kinder-garten written to various people in Froebel's life. Interesting view of Froebel's philosophy from a more personal perspective.
87. *Autobiographie Und Kliener Schriften.* Berlin: W. Lange, 1892. [*Autobiog-raphy of Friedrich Froebel.* Trans. Emilie Michaelis and H. Keatley Moore. Syracuse: C.W. Bardeen, 1889.] Presents personal insights, memories, and the development of his philosophy. A good view of Froebel which assists in an understanding of his ideas.
88. *Education by Development.* Trans. Josephine Jarvis. New York: D. Appleton & Co., 1899. Describes child development as an unfolding process. An attempt to explain this part of Froebel's philosophy to teachers.
89. *Friedrich Wilhelm August Froebel Gesammelte Padagogiche Schriften* herausgegeben (edited by) von Wilhard Lange 2Tle. in 3. Berlin: T. C. F. Enslin, 1862-1863. [Complete Educational Writings, edited by Wichard Lang] [*Froebel's Chief Writings on Education* Rendered into English by S. S. Fletcher & J. Welton. New York: Longmans, Green & Co., 1912.] Presents Froebel's most widely read material on education in one place.

SECONDARY SOURCES

90. Barnard, Henry, ed. *The Kindergarten and Child Culture Papers.* Hartford: Office of Barnard's American Journal of Education, 1890. A collection of articles by American and European experts on Froebel's theory and prac-tice intended to publicize the kindergarten. Excellent historical sources.
91. Frost, Ilse. *The Early Years at School.* New York: McGraw-Hill, 1949. Bib-liography and interpretation of Froebel's work in the context of twentieth-century practice. Brief historical discussion.
92. Frost, Ilse. *Preschool Education: A Historical and Critical Study.* New York: Macmillan, 1929. Discussion of the roots of early childhood education. Describes the value of concepts in Froebel's theory; the value of play; Froebel's ideas concerning early education in the home; the education of women; certain of Froebel's theories which tend to inhibit the desirable growth of the kindergarten institution; and the influence of Froebel's edu-cational ideas on the development of early kindergartens. Extensive bibli-ography.
93. Kilpatrick, William Heard. *Froebel's Kindergarten Principles Critically Examined.* New York: Macmillan, 1916. Excellent critique and analysis

of Froebel's writings, theory, and practice. This analysis gave ammunition to the Progressive group within the International Kindergarten Union because Kilpatrick found psychological deficiencies in Froebel's theory advocating habit formation as an alternative and as essential for proper development.

94. Lazerson, Marvin. "The Historical Antecedents of Early Childhood Education." In *Early Childhood Education: Seventy-First Yearbook of the National Society for the Study of Education,* ed. Ira J. Gordon. Chicago: University of Chicago Press, 1972, pp. 33-35. Traces the history of early childhood education with a clear discussion of Froebel's work; includes a bibliography.

95. Ulich, Robert. *History of Educational Thought.* New York: American Book Co., 1968. Good analysis of Froebel's philosophy of unity and philosophy of education with an excellent bibliography of primary and secondary sources.

96. Ulich, Robert. *Three Thousand Years of Educational Wisdom: Selections from Great Documents.* Cambridge: Harvard University Press, 1954; rev. ed. 1982, pp. 523-576. Brief discussion of Froebel's theory and practice with excerpts from *The Autobiography* and *The Education of Man.* Useful introduction to primary sources.

97. Von Marenholtz-Bulow, Bertha. *Reminiscence of Freidrich Froebel.* Trans. Mrs. Horace Mann. Boston: Lothrop, Less & Shepard Co., 1905. Presents personal memories of training by one of Froebel's students.

98. Weber, Evelyn. *The Kindergarten: Its Encounter with Educational Thought in America.* New York: Teachers College Press, 1969. Excellent analysis and discussion of Froebel's philosophy and practice in chapter 1. Excellent bibliography of primary and secondary sources.

99. Wheelock, Lucy, and Caroline D. Aborn, eds. *The Kindergarten in New England.* Washington, D.C.: Association for Childhood Education, 1935. A discussion of the historical development and progress (up to 1935) of the kindergarten in the New England states with comments about ACE activities and local associations activities in each state.

100. Wheelock, Lucy, Caroline D. Aborn, and Sarah A. Marble, eds. *History of the Kindergarten Movement in the Mid-Western States and in New York.* Washington, D.C.: Association for Childhood Education, 1938. Presents the history and progress of the kindergarten (up to 1938) in the midwestern states and New York State with comments on the activities of kindergarten associations.

101. Wheelock, Lucy, and Barbara Greenwood, eds. *History of the Kindergarten Movement in the Western States, Hawaii and Alaska.* Washington, D.C.: Association for Childhood Education, 1940. Describes the progress (up to 1940) of the kindergarten movement in the western states, including the territories Alaska and Hawaii. Provides material by experts from each state. Excellent view of the progress of the establishment of kindergartens

and the start of early childhood education throughout America.

102. Wheelock, Lucy, and Catherine R. Watkins, eds. *History of the Kindergarten Movement in the Southeastern States and Delaware, District of Columbia, New Jersey, and Pennsylvania.* Washington, D.C.: Association for Childhood Education, 1939. Traces the history of the kindergarten in the southeastern states with a discussion of activities (up to 1939) by the kindergarten associations.

Arnold Lucius Gesell (1880-1961)

As G. Stanley Hall's most famous student, Gesell built on his mentor's work by introducing the use of one way mirrors and cinematography to child study. Gesell advocated a "downward extension" of education to include children considered too young for kindergarten. Enthusiasm for nursery school education was encouraged by Gesell's articles in *Childhood Education.*

Gesell's contributions to early childhood education include a new view of how children grow and develop based on film and photographic samples of behavior; respect for individual differences in development; use of age characteristics and interests to plan curriculum and activities; and a commitment to the importance of the ages 2 through 6 in the life of a child.

Without Gesell's work in child study, early childhood education would not have been able to move toward recognizing and meeting the needs of all young children.

PRIMARY SOURCES

103. "The Changing Status of the Pre-School Child." *Progressive Education* 2 (January-March, 1925): 8-10. Discusses increased interest in the preschool child (providing a definition of the age group), new trends in legislation, education, home life, public health practices, and clinic and laboratory practices. Describes medical, educational, legislative, and child study practices that make preschool education an exciting idea.

104. *The Mental Growth of the Pre-School Child: A Psychological Outline of Normal Development from Birth to the Sixth Year, Including a System of Developmental Diagnosis.* New York: Macmillan, 1925. A detailed description of every aspect of child development from birth to age 6. Includes 200 photographs.

105. "The Significance of the Nursery School." *Childhood Education* 1, no. 1 (September 1925): 11-22. Discusses the nursery school movement in terms of the origin of the nursery school, the educational significance of the preschool period, the mental hygiene of the preschool age, the social control of preschool hygiene, and the social significance of the nursery school. Concludes by stating that nursery school education must preserve the parent-child relationship and not place too much emphasis on the child as a child.

106. "The Downward Extension of the Kindergarten: A Unified Policy for Early Education." *Childhood Education* 2, no. 2 (October, 1926): 53-59. Provides historical information about the kindergarten and nursery school as

the basis for an integrated, unified early childhood education. Provides evidence from educational practice, psychology, and child development to show that early childhood education must use the developmental opportunities available to all children starting from infancy. The unified education will help the exceptional child and the average child reach his/her potential in all developmental areas.

107.   *The Guidance of Mental Growth in Infant and Child.* New York: Macmillan, 1930. Presents information on the problems and methods of developmental guidance. Part I presents an historical discussion of child development in the eighteenth and nineteenth centuries, a discussion of the nursery school movement, and the reconstruction of the kindergarten, and the role of the kindergarten in mental hygiene and preschool education. Part II discusses the stages and norms of mental growth, the parent-child relationship, and early diagnoses of developmental defects. Part III discusses research in child development, heredity and mental growth, and the medical aspects of the study of infant behavior. Photographs include a pictorial history of child life, showing engravings from old books for children, stages of infant growth and behavior; a view of supervised child development; a view of a guidance nursery; and a view of the Yale Psycho-Clinic Guidance Nursery.

108.   "The Yale Clinic of Child Development." *Childhood Education* 8 (May 1932): 468-469. Describes the function, research goals, affiliation, and collaborative efforts of the clinic with pediatric, psychiatric, and psychology departments of the university in 1932.

109.   and Helen Thompson. Assisted by Catherine Strunk Amatruda. *The Psychology of Early Growth: Including Norms of Infant Behavior and a Method of Genetic Analysis.* New York: Macmillan, 1938. An update of the 1925 study (see no. 104) of infant development based on ten years of additional research. Describes the methods of the study, norms of infant growth, and the analytic appraisal of growth status. Includes a glossary and bibliography of Yale films on child development.

110.   *The First Five Years of Life: A Guide to the Study of the Preschool Child.* Part I by Arnold Gesell. Part II by Henry M. Halverson, Helen Thompson, Frances Ilg, Burton Castner, and Louise Bates Ames. Part III by Arnold Gesell and Catherine Amatruda. New York: Harper & Row, 1940. A study of the intellect, language, social adaptive behavior (problem solving, memory, and drawing), and motor development of the child from birth to age 5. There are twenty-one pages of photographs showing development at every stage, including children's drawings, attempts at writing, and outdoor play. There also are pictures of preschool materials and the nursery at the Yale Clinic of Child Development.

111.   and Frances L. Ilg, in collaboration with Louise Bates Ames and Glenna E. Bullis, *The Child from Five to Ten.* New York: Harper & Row, 1946. Describes the social, physical, emotional, intellectual, and language development from age 5 to age 10. There is material on fears and dreams,

play and school life.

112. "Arnold L. Gesell." In *History of Psychology in Autobiography,* eds. E. Boring, H. Langfeld, R. Yerkes, and Heinz Werner. Volume 4. Worcester: Clark University Press, 1952, pp. 123-142. An autobiography with a discussion of Gesell's early life and work at the Yale Clinic.

SECONDARY SOURCES

113. Ames, Louise Bates. *Arnold Gesell, Themes of His Work.* New York: Human Sciences, Press, 1989. A detailed discussion of the themes Gesell investigated in his research with reference to specific articles and books in each theme. The themes include school readiness, social needs, child health, vision, kindergarten, nursery school, parenting, a history of the Gesell Institute, and evaluations of Gesell's work. An extensive bibliography is included.

114. Ames, Louise Bates. "Dr. Arnold Gesell 1880-1961." *British Journal of Educational Psychology* 32 (June 1962): 101-102. A tribute to Gesell summarizing his contributions to the field of child development by his colleague.

115. "Arnold Gesell Dies." *New York Times,* May 30, 1961, p. 17. An obituary discussing Gesell's life and work at Yale.

116. "Dr. Gesell, Famed Child Expert Dies." *New Haven Register,* May 29, 1961, pp. 1 & 3. An obituary discussing Gesell's life and work with a partial list of publications.

117. Gross, Miriam Zeller. "Men of Medicine: He Made a Science of Child Development." *Postgraduate Medicine* 13, no. 2 (February 1953): 179-184. Provides biographical information discussed in the context of Gesell's contributions to child development. Gesell's portrait is included on page 180.

118. Lindley, Pamela Garland. "Dr. Arnold Lucius Gesell: Philosopher, Child Psychologist, Pediatrician, Clinical Researcher." Ph.D. Diss.,. Texas Woman's University, 1991. Presents a discussion of Gesell's contributions to child development and the relevance of his theories to modern child study. Contains biographical material, a bibliography of primary and secondary sources, and the contents of Gesell's papers.

119. Miles, Walter R. "Arnold Lucius Gesell 1880-1961: A Biographical Memoir." In *Biographical Memoirs.* Washington, D.C.: National Academy of Sciences, 1964, Vol. 37, pp. 55-96. A detailed biography and discussion of Gesell's work, including a bibliography of primary sources from 1905 to 1959. A photograph of Gesell with his signature are included.

120. "New Member of the Laureate Chapter." *Kappa Delta Pi Forum* 22, no. 4 (May 1958): 504j. Announces Gesell's installation as a member of the Laureate Chapter of Kappa Delta Pi. Provides brief biographical information and a list of primary sources (titles and dates).

121. Weber, Evelyn. *Ideas Influencing Early Childhood Education: A Theoretical Analysis.* New York: Teachers College Press, 1984, pp. 54-61. A detailed analysis of Gesell's work in the context of early childhood education. Discusses Gesell's ages and stages; a child's readiness for learning; and the influence of the normative view.

122. Weber, Evelyn. *The Kindergarten: Its Encounter with Educational Thought in America.* New York: Teachers College Press, 1969, pp. 172-179. Discusses Gesell's work as a student of Hall and the significance of his contributions to child study for the kindergarten movement and early childhood education.

William Nicholas Hailmann (1836-1920)

Translator of Froebel's *The Education of Man,* Hailmann worked for the establishment of kindergartens in America.

Hailmann undertook a study of kindergartens in Zurich and was director of the German-American Academy in Louisville, Kentucky, the German-American Academy in Milwaukee, Wisconsin, and the German-American Seminary in Detroit, Michigan. He served as superintendent of schools in LaPorte, Indiana. With his wife, Eudora, he established kindergartens, trained teachers, and advocated the study of art and manual training in all the cities in which he worked. He was elected leader of the Froebel Institute of North America; first President of the Kindergarten Department of the National Education Association; and from 1894-1898, he served as Federal Supervisor of Indian Schools in Washington, D.C., establishing kindergartens and teacher training schools. He held positions as supervisor of Dayton, Ohio schools; head of the psychology department at Chicago Normal School (which became Chicago State University); professor of the history of education at Cleveland Normal Training School in Ohio; and professor at Broadoaks Kindergarten Normal School in Pasadena, California. Hailmann organized the Kindergarten-Primary Council of the West in California, received the Bicknell Prize from the American Institute of Instruction for *The Application of Psychology to the Work of Teaching;* and was editor of *Erziehungsblatter* from 1870-1873, as well as *The Kindergarten Messenger* and *New Education* from 1876-1883.

Hailmann worked for modification of Frederich Froebel's theory in response to American social conditions because "no theory can take into consideration the manifold differences that beset practice."

PRIMARY SOURCES

123. "Adaptation of Froebel's System of Education to American Institutions." *National Education Association Journal of Proceedings and Addresses, 1872.* Illinois: N.C. Nason Printer, 1873, pp. 141-147; discussion, pp. 147-174. States that systems of education must adapt to varying circumstances. Suggests that modification in application of Froebel's theory, activities, and materials should be made to correspond to the nature and needs of American children and American social circumstances. Educators must look at each child as an individual and a member of a society and adapt methods and materials to children's needs.
124. *Kindergarten Culture in the Family and Kindergarten.* New York: American Book Co., 1873. Discusses the application of Froebel's aims and methods

in the kindergarten classroom and at home by parents. Discusses the Mother Play and songs and the value of the kindergarten for all children.

125. "The Kindergarten Exhibit." *National Education Association Journal of Proceedings and Addresses 1885 at Saratoga Springs, New York.* New York: Little & Co., 1886, pp. 546-551. Describes the children's work displayed at an international exhibit of kindergarten work in New Orleans, criticizing most of the work for its "random character…indicated that the schools failed to appreciate the meaning and value of the material." He called most of what he saw busy work, but cited Clinton, Iowa; Grand Rapids, Michigan; and LaPorte, Indiana; as showing an organic connection between hard work, materials, and school work, showing a systematic use of the materials for "legitimate school purposes." Praised the use of drawing. Stated that kindergarten work should not be used in the primary school to keep children busy, but should be used to intensify and strengthen content instruction. Lists the strengths of the LaPorte display and praises the State Normal School at Winona, Minnesota, for the truly American spirit of their work showing originality. Describes the French and Japanese exhibits. States that the exhibit as a whole shows the progress of the kindergarten from isolation to a friendly companionship to the other educational levels.

126. "Kindergarten Instruction: President Hailmann's Address." *National Education Association Journal of Proceedings and Addresses 1885 Held at Saratoga Springs, New York.* New York: Little & Co., 1886, pp. 349-350. The opening address of the first session of the Kindergarten Department of the NEA. Hailmann lists the two main problems that the department will attempt to solve as (1) What are the principles and methods the kindergarten uses to arouse children's interest in life and their environment and develop skills? and (2) To what extent do these principles and methods apply to school life? What modifications are needed in the aims to make the kindergarten a happy place for a child to grow in body and soul? States that the task is difficult and will take time and study beyond the kindergarten manual to a broad view of art and science. Sets the platform for further inquiry.

127. *Primary Methods and Kindergarten Instruction: A Complete and Methodological Presentation of the Use of Kindergarten Materials in the Work of the Primary School Unfolding a Systematic Course of Manual Training in Connection with Arithmetic, Geometry, Drawing, and Other School Subjects.* New York: A.S. Barnes, 1887. Describes in detail the use of Friedrich Froebel's methods and materials in the primary grades to enhance instruction and provide for individual growth and skill mastery.

128. "Report of Committee on Hygiene in Education. Harmonious Development." *National Education Association Journal of Proceedings and Addresses, 1889.* Topeka: Kansas Publishing House, 1889, pp. 404-416. Discusses harmony as an educational principle. Describes static and dynamic har-

monies, the task of education in harmonious development, Friedrich Froebel's philosophy, and how education can help children achieve harmonious development. States that the road to harmonious development goes through obedience and leads the child to freedom and mastery. Education's business is to lead "to this harmony the being of every human child in a persistently and consistently all sided harmonious practice."

129. *The Education of Man Translated and Annotated from Froebel's Die Menschen Erziehung.* New York: D. Appleton & Co., 1889; New York: Augustus M. Kellet, 1970. (repr.) Presents Froebel's philosophical creed, the importance of play, and the philosophy on which his theory of early childhood education is based. Froebel's title should have been translated *The Education of People.*

130. "Schoolishness in the Kindergarten." *National Education Association Journal of Proceedings and Addresses, 1890.* Topeka: Kansas Publishing House, 1890, pp. 565-573. Discusses the reasons why the kindergarten should not follow the "schoolishness" of the primary school. States that Froebel's aims are not those of the primary grades. Provides examples of children being pushed into reading, writing, and arithmetic at the kindergarten level, causing the neglect of the imaginative, spontaneous, creative experiences that achieve "joyous interest…and achievements in productive or creative tendency and skill in life efficiency." States that rather than allowing the child to develop at his/her own pace in an unhurried atmosphere, many superintendents, such as William T. Harris, are justifying the shift to academic instruction and the dismissal of play in favor of conventional instruction. This discussion sounds like a very contemporary argument against hurrying children for the sake of early academic gains. David Elkind would agree with Hailmann.

131. "Manual Training in the Elementary School." *National Education Association Journal of Proceedings and Addresses, Held at Saint Paul, Minnesota, 1890.* Topeka: Kansas Publishing House, 1890, pp. 842-850. States that manual training should not be one-sided training that emphasizes only skill training or only aesthetic outcomes and neglects the other aspects of education. The purpose of educative manual training is not art alone or artisanship alone, "but a union of the two in a life of conscious, intelligent, world-absorption and self-expansion…of self harmony with other forces…and social endeavor." Manual training in the elementary school should follow the needs of the child's cognitive development at each stage. The program should appeal to analytical or discriminating processes at first developing observational skills and move to the application of knowledge to develop productive, inventive, and creative activities. States that Froebel divided products into forms that bring knowledge (science in the elementary school); and forms that represent or help life (utility or industrial activities in the elementary school); and forms that gratify the sense of harmony and beauty (in the elementary school, this is artistic self-ex-

pression). States that manual training should not be a subject by itself which makes the acquisition of skill its aim. It is a means, not an end.

132. "The Kindergarten Occupations." *The Proceedings of the Thirteenth Annual Meeting of The International Kindergarten Union, 1906*, pp. 88-98; *Kindergarten Review* (June, 1906): 39-44. Enumerates the principles that Froebel used to select and guide the use of occupations with children. States that the choice of occupations depends on the interest and needs of the individual child. The child's initiative should be considered, but he/she may lose interest if asked to work on an occupation for which he/she is not yet developmentally ready. Criticizes the practice of having all children working on the same activity at the same time, stating that teachers need to evaluate and consider each child's ability and stage of development before suggesting materials. There is a need to coordinate activities and literature.

SECONDARY SOURCES

133. Beatty, Barbara "Child Gardening: The Teaching of Young Children in American Schools." In *American Teachers: Histories of a Profession at Work*, ed. Donald Warren. New York: Macmillan, 1989, pp. 65-97. Describes the kindergarten movement and the contributions of pioneers, including Hailmann, who emphasized the harmony, wholeness, and continuity of Froebel's philosophy. States that Hailmann opposed the idea that the kindergarten was the same as school and stated that teachers should not use activities intended for older children.

134. Doeflinger, Charles H. "The Kindergarten Movement in Milwaukee." *Kindergarten Magazine* 18 (March 1906): 385-406. Presents the history of the kindergarten in Milwaukee, describing Hailmann's contribution to the development of the kindergarten in America.

135. Greenwood, Barbara. "William Nicholas Hailmann." In *Pioneers of the Kindergarten in America. Prepared by the Committee of Nineteen, The International Kindergarten Union.* New York: The Century Co., 1924, pp. 245-262. A biographical memoir with a discussion of William and Eudora Hailmann's work in teacher training. The influence on changes in classroom materials and activities to promote a freer social interaction among children is discussed, along with the Hailmann's many contributions to the kindergarten movement.

136. "Hailmann, William Nicholas." In *Biographical Dictionary of American Educators*, vol. 2, ed. John F. Ohles. Westport Connecticut: Greenwood Press, 1978, pp. 575-576. A biography listing Hailmann's major publications and contributions to the kindergarten movement as first chairman of the NEA Kindergarten Department, his work with Native Americans, and his work in California as the organizer of the Kindergarten-Primary Council of the West.

137. "Hailmann, William Nicholas." In *Dictionary of American Biography.* vol. 8, ed. Dumas Malone. New York: Scribner's Sons, 1932, pp. 90-91. A biographical sketch including a list of Hailmann's publications, a discussion of his work in the kindergarten movement, the NEA, and as superintendent of Indian Education.

138. "Hailmann, William Nicholas." In *Who Was Who in America with World Notables,* vol. 4, 5th ed. Chicago: Marquis Who's Who Inc., 1968, p. 393. A very short biographical sketch including publications.

139. Hewes, Dorothy. "Early Childhood Commercial Exhibit Controversies: 1890 and 1980." ERIC Document ED330431. Paper presented at NAEYC History Seminar, Washington, D.C., November 16, 1990. Describes the controversy between early childhood education ethics and principles and the commercial exhibits at the 1990 NAEYC meeting. Research indicates that William and Eudora Hailmann opposed dictated activities found in books published by Milton Bradley and E. Steiger and advocated developmental freedom. Hewes states that Hailmann and the Froebelian kindergarten appear to have had little influence on American education in the late twentieth century because of the existing commercialism that he opposed.

140. Hewes, Dorothy. "Organic Education in Public Schools of Late Nineteenth Century America." ERIC Document ED299048. Paper presented at the International Standing Conference for the History of Education 10th Session, Joensuu, Finland, July 27, 1988. States that organic education was based on Froebel's idea of life as a connected whole and favored self-activity and self-direction in a child-centered classroom. This was in opposition to John Locke's concept of the child as a blank slate on which teachers were to impress the virtues of good citizenship. One hundred years after Hailmann introduced organic education into the LaPorte, Indiana, schools the issue of incorporating organic education into the public schools is again being debated.

141. Hewes, Dorothy. "Those First Good Years of Indian Education: 1894-1898." *American Indian Culture and Research Journal* 5, no. 2 (1981). 63-82. Describes the curriculum implemented by Hailmann as Superintendent of Indian Schools based on Froebel's philosophy with elements of the 1960s open education plan.

142. Hewes, Dorothy. *W. N. Hailmann Defender of Froebel.* Ph.D. diss., Union Graduate School, Yellow Springs, Ohio, 1974. A most comprehensive discussion of Hailmann's life and work in America as the interpreter and defender of Froebel. Includes a list of Hailmann's publications and endnotes and a bibliography of primary and secondary sources. A "Synoptical of Gifts and Occupations" from *The Education of Man,* tracing the development of the materials, also is included. This is the best work on Hailmann's contributions to education.

143. "In Dr. Hailmann's Behalf." *New York Times,* January 24, 1897, p. 3, col. 2. A report of a petition to President-elect William McKinley requesting the

reappointment of Hailmann as Superintendent of Indian Schools. Praises Hailmann's ability as "unquestionably the ablest educator who ever had charge of this branch of work." The letter is signed by prominent educators and the Indian Rights Association. The signitors also include Theodore Roosevelt, Seth Low, W. E. Dodge, and James MacAlester.

144. "New Elementary School on Ohio Street Named in Memory of Dr. W. Hailmann. Educator Founded Kindergarten Here in Autumn of 1889." *The LaPorte Herald-Argus,* July 7, 1955, p. 1. Announces the name of the new elementary school will honor the memory of Dr. William Nicholas Hailmann, founder of the second kindergarten west of the Alleghenies in 1889. Provides biographical information about Hailmann including a photograph taken in the 1880s and information about the training school he and Eudora Hailmann organized. States that in 1936 LaPorte celebrated the 50th anniversary of the founding of the free public kindergarten by Hailmann. States that "school officials believe that the action to honor Dr. Hailmann taken by the board this week consummates an obligation on the part of the LaPorte community that has long been overdue."

145. Ross, Elizabeth Dale. *The Kindergarten Crusade: The Establishment of Preschool Education in the United States.* Ohio: University of Ohio Press, 1976, pp. 10, 37-38, 63, 70, 87-88. Discusses Hailmann's contributions to the kindergarten movement with emphasis on his efforts to spread the kindergarten into the public school system and his life-long commitment to the benefits of the kindergarten for all children.

146. Shapiro, Michael Steven. *Child's Garden: The Kindergarten Movement from Froebel to Dewey.* University Park: The Pennsylvania State University Press, 1983, pp. 29-30, 67, 135, 140, 151. Brief discussion of Hailmann's work in the kindergarten movement, his chairmanship of the NEA Kindergarten Department, and his support for the reform of schools and the place of the kindergarten in schools.

147. Vanderwalker, Nina C. *The Kindergarten in American Education.* New York: Macmillan, 1908; New York: Arno Press & The New York Times, 1971, (repr.) pp. 13, 17, 21-23, 30-33, 36. Describes Hailmann's work to establish the kindergarten in America. Discusses his visit to the Zurich schools in 1860; the establishment of the kindergarten in the German-American Academy in Louisville; the German-English Academy in Milwaukee in 1874, when Hailmann became the president; the training classes for teachers; and his work in the NEA. States that Hailmann became editor of the *New Education,* which was very influential in shaping policy and developing interest in the kindergarten in the Northwest. Praises Hailmann's efforts.

148. Weber, Evelyn. *The Kindergarten. Its Encounter with Educational Thought in America.* New York: Teachers College Press, 1969, pp. 3, 12, 20, 33-34, 42, 46, 65-66. Discussion of Hailmann's work in the NEA and as a pioneer in the kindergarten movement. Provides a bibliography of primary and secondary sources.

149. Wesley, Edgar B. *NEA: The First Hundred Years; The Building of the Teaching Profession.* New York: Harper & Brothers, 1957, pp. 158, 160-162, 191. Discusses Hailmann's role as first president of the NEA Kindergarten Department in 1884 and 1894 president of the Elementary School Department. Describes Hailmann's life and work, referring to his many publications in the NEA journal. Provides specific information about the topics discussed by the Kindergarten Department during its long history which worked with the International Kindergarten Union (founded in 1892).

Granville Stanley Hall (1844-1924)

Hall laid the foundation for modern child psychology and helped to reshape the kindergarten.

The contributions Hall made to early childhood education include the creation of the child study movement; a curriculum based on the nature and needs of children as gathered by objective observational techniques; clean, well-lit, well-ventilated classrooms for kindergartens; and, because large muscles develop early and need exercise, a program of active games, music, spontaneous free play, language development, outdoor play, and the use of the imagination to replace Froebel's sedentary activities that overused immature small muscles. He encouraged teachers to experiment with methods and materials; as first president of Clark University, he developed a series of summer conferences to enable teachers to discuss problems in child development that attracted leaders in kindergarten reform; which created a controversy and a split in the International Kindergarten Union that led to reforms. He also developed questionnaires and anecdotal records as methods of data collection; enlisted teachers in data collection on physical, intellectual, emotional, and social behavior; concluded that children think and react differently from adults; believed in an evolutionary concept of development that each stage must be lived through for development to be complete. He was the author of many books and articles including *The Content of Children's Minds*.

The child study movement helped kindergarten theory and practice evolve into valuable contributions to education. New insights into how young children learn and what they are able to do became the basis for educational practice at all levels.

PRIMARY SOURCES

150. "The Content of Children's Minds." *Princeton Review* 2 (May 1883): 249-272. First major work based on data gathered by teachers in Boston. Interesting tabulation of questions.

151. "New Departures in Education." *The North American Review* 140 (February 1885): 144-152. States that the common school does not respect childhood. Provides advice on restructuring school to include a new education based on a knowledge of childhood.

152. "The Story of a Sand Pile." *Scribner's Magazine* 3 (June 1888): pp. 690-696. Describes children at play in a longitudinal study, which is not his usual research method. Reports how children playing alone create their own social institutions providing evidence that children's development can be seen as the basis for socialization. This has been called Hall's most

charming essay on children. Uses observation in a natural setting to collect data. He was well ahead of his time because the method was not perfected until much later in the twentieth century.

153. "Boy Life in a Massachusetts Country Town Thirty Years Ago." *Proceedings of the American Antiquarian Society* 7 (1891): 107-128. Hall recalls how wonderful it was to learn from nature on a Massachusetts farm. Advises that the old-fashioned life was best for children. Insight into Hall's belief that natural education was best and children of the 1890s were being cheated because of urbanization. A romantic view of farm life.

154. "From Fundamental to Accessory in Education." *Kindergarten Magazine* 11 (May 1899): 556-600. Discussion of the development of small and large muscles and the right approach in education to avoid their overuse and misuse.

155. "Some Defects in the Kindergarten in America." *The Forum* 28 (January 1900): 579-591. A discussion of problems and abuses in kindergarten practice with information on health conditions.

156. "Child Study and its Relation to Education." *The Forum* 29 (August 1900): 688-693, 696-702. A defense of child study and its value for psychology and education that respects children's nature and needs. Acknowledges the weaknesses of child study, but believes that it has the ultimate power to change educational practices for all ages. There is information on adolescence which would, four years later, become a major interest for Hall.

157. "The Ideal School as Based on Child Study." *National Education Association Journal of Addresses and Proceedings, 1901,* pp. 475-488; *The Forum* 32 (1901-1902): 24-39. This is Hall's most important statement on education. An outline of educational practice from kindergarten to high school emphasizing a child-centered, slow process with respect for health, growth, and heredity. A detailed, well-organized plan for school reform using child study as its foundation.

158. "Address to the National Education Association." *Kindergarten Review,* September, 1901, pp. 12, 43-46. Discusses abuses and misuses of occupations in kindergartens.

159. *Adolescence: Its Psychology and its Relations to Physiology, Anthropology, Sociology, Sex, Crime, Religion, and Education.* Vols. 1,2. New York: D. Appleton & Company, 1904, pp.viii-xix. A major work discussing the contrast between the savage child and the civilized adolescent. Tries to relate psychology to education and social reform and outlines a concept of child development that is the most characteristic of his ideas. States that high school should be the most important part of the new education. Full of opinions and facts with some very antifeminist views on the education of girls.

160. *Aspects of Child Life and Education by Stanley Hall and Some of His Pupils.* ed. by Theodore Smith. New York: Ginn & Co., 1907, ii-ix by Hall. Describes briefly the whole thesis of genetic psychology and the cultural epoch theory.

161. *Educational Problems.* Vol. 1. New York: D. Appleton, 1911, pp. 1-41. A complete discussion of "the Pedagogy of the Kindergarten" discussing the ideal kindergarten; Friedrich Froebel's defects; the need for transcribing Froebel's limitations; Caroline Burk's experiments with free play; Susan Blow's criticism of Dopp, John Dewey, and G. Stanley Hall; the kindergarten in Europe; the need and lack of child study for the kindergarten age; specific reforms needed; the progressive and conservative schools; and kindergarten's relations to the day nursery. This is Hall's second major two volume work.

162. *Life and Confessions of a Psychologist.* New York: D Appleton & Company, 1923. An autobiography with a discussion of educational changes, the development of child study, his work at Johns Hopkins, and the founding of Clark University. Good background information.

SECONDARY SOURCES

163. Ambron, Sueann Robinson, and David Brodzinsky. *Life Span Development.* New York: Holt, Rinehart and Winston, 1982, pp. 221-239. A description of physical and perceptual development in the preschool years through age 5.

164. Averill, Lawrence A. "Recollections of Clarke's G. Stanley Hall." *Journal of the History of the Behavioral Sciences* 18 (January 1982): 341-346. A personal perspective by a 1915 doctoral student who studied with Hall. Good insight into Hall as teacher and advisor.

165. Cremin, Lawrence A. *American Education: The Metropolitan Experience 1876-1980.* New York: Harper and Row, 1988, pp. 278-280, 305-307, 309, 557, 558. Excellent bibliographic essay and discussion of Hall's impact on educational practices.

166. Cremin, Lawrence A. *The Transformation of the Schools: Progressivism in American Education 1876-1957.* New York: Knopf, 1961, pp. 100-107. A brief, well-written description of Hall's work with emphasis on his philosophy.

167. Curti, Merle. *The Social Ideas of American Education.* New Jersey: Littlefield, Adams and Co., 1966, pp. 396-428. Discussion of Hall's life and work. Bibliography is difficult to use as it has some incomplete and very old sources cited, however, it is worth consulting.

168. Dozier, Cynthia. "Roundtable Conference on Supervision." *Proceedings of the Eighth Annual Convention of the International Kindergarten Union,* April 10-13, 1901. Chicago, Illinois. Dubuque, IA: Union Printing Co., 1907. Report of many aspects of kindergarten practice including the importance of health condition.

169. Hoxie, Jane. "The Development of Occupations." *Proceedings of the Seventeenth Annual Meeting of the International Kindergarten Union,* April 27-29, 1910. St. Louis, Missouri. Woburn, Mass.: Andrews Printing Co., 1910. Describes problems found in the use of Froebel's occupations.

170. Jones, Hortense P., et al. "Child Development Focus." In *Minimum Teaching Essentials Grades K-9*, ed. New York City Board of Education: Office of Curriculum Development and Support, Division of Curriculum and Instruction, 1980, pp. 89-92. An outline of the physical, social, emotional, and intellectual characteristics of elementary school pupils grades K-9. Useful source.

171. Lazerson, Marvin. "The Historical Antecedents of Early Childhood Education." In *Early Childhood Education, The Seventy-First Yearbook of the National Society for the Study of Education*, ed. Ira J. Gordon. Illinois: University of Chicago Press, 1972, pp. 33-53. Relates Hall's educational philosophy to the beginnings of early childhood education. A brief discussion.

172. Martindell, Charlotte Sherwood, "New Developments in Kindergarten Work." *Kindergarten Review* 9 (February 1899): 358-361. Discusses the need for free expression in art. This was new at the time since all kindergarten work followed prescribed, teacher-directed products.

173. New York State Education Department. *The Elementary School Curriculum: An Overview.* Albany: Bureau of Elementary Curriculum Development, 1954, pp. 15-30. Describes the kindergarten child and the content of the kindergarten curriculum.

174. Poulsson, Emilie. "The Story." *Proceedings of the Fifteenth Annual Meeting of the International Kindergarten Union*, March 30-31 and April 1-2, 1908, New Orleans. Rochester, New York: E. R. Andrews Publishing Co., 1908. Discussion of the use of literature for young children.

175. Ross, Dorothy. *G. Stanley Hall: The Psychologist as Prophet.* Chicago: University of Chicago Press, 1972. Biography of Hall with a good bibliography and a chronological list of Hall's written work.

176. Sargent, Walter. "The Beginnings of Art in the Kindergarten." In *Proceedings of the Seventeenth Annual Meeting of the International Kindergarten Union*, April 27-29, 1910. St. Louis, Missouri. Woburn, Mass.: Andrews Publishing Co., 1910. Discussion of how children draw and why they need freedom of expression rather than teacher direction. Interesting and worth reading even today for insight into children's forms of expression.

177. Shapiro, Michael Steven. *Child's Garden: The Kindergarten Movement from Froebel to Dewey.* University Park: Pennsylvania State University Press, 1983, pp. 107-130. Discussion of the child study movement and Hall's contributions to changes in kindergarten practice. Useful bibliography.

178. Snyder, Agness. *Dauntless Women in Childhood Education, 1856-1931.* Washington, D.C.: Association for Childhood Education International, 1972, pp. 178-181. A very brief discussion of the importance of child study to the Progressive kindergarten movement.

179. Strickland, Charles E. and Burgess, Charles. *Health, Growth and Heredity, G. Stanley Hall on Education.* New York: Teachers College Press, 1965.

Profile of Hall with twelve excerpts from his writing. Preface by Lawrence A. Cremin. A good source of a variety of Hall's best-known writings.

180. Vanderwalker, Nina C. "The History of Kindergarten Influence in Elementary Education." In *The Sixth Yearbook of the National Society for the Scientific Study of Education: Part II. The Kindergarten and Its Relations to Elementary Education,* ed. Manfred J. Holmes. Illinois: Public School Publishing Co., 1907, pp. 115-133. Discussion of many aspects of kindergarten theory and practice including information on genetic psychology and child study written by a teacher trainer in the kindergarten department of the then State Normal School in Milwaukee.

181. Weber, Evelyn. *The Kindergarten: Its Encounter with Educational Thought in America.* New York: Teachers College, Press, 1969, pp. 48-51, 54-58, 84, 90, 99, 120, 125, 167, 172, 176. Discusses Hall's influence on kindergarten curriculum, methods and materials. Extensive bibliography. An excellent source.

William Torrey Harris (1835-1908) and Susan E. Blow (1843-1916)

Under the leadership of Superintendent of Schools Harris and teacher-trainer Blow, the first free kindergarten to be part of a large urban public school system opened in St. Louis in 1873.

The contributions made by Harris and Blow to early childhood education include lowering the school entrance age to provide a longer period of education for the urban poor; combining theory and actual classroom practice with exposure to the liberal arts in a teacher training program; clear and inspired interpretations of Friedrich Froebel's work; the acceptance of the kindergarten as part of public school education; the spread of the kindergarten movement throughout the United States; and the training of many future leaders and teacher educators in early childhood education. Blow was a leader in the International Kindergarten Union and the Committee of Nineteen; and Harris served as United States Commissioner of Education (1886-1906). In addition, Blow was an influential author and lecturer at Teachers' College, Columbia University.

The combined leadership of Harris and Blow made St. Louis a national model for the development of public school kindergartens and the training of kindergarten teachers.

PRIMARY SOURCES—HARRIS

182. "The Kindergarten." In *Twenty-Second Annual Report of the Board of Directors of the St. Louis Public Schools Year Ending August 1, 1876*, St. Louis: Slowson Printers, 1877, pp. 79-119. Presents a history of the kindergarten experiment in the St. Louis Public Schools describing its benefits to the poor, costs, teacher training, Blow's work, attendance, curriculum, teachers' salary, play, dangers in classroom management techniques, Froebel's Gifts and Occupations with illustrations for each, success in primary school after the kindergarten experience supported by statistics, and the kindergarten "Americanized." Presents a great deal of information. Concludes with questions about the kindergarten that need further consideration.

183. "Psychological Inquiry." *National Education Association Journal of Proceedings and Addresses, 1885 at Saratoga Springs, New York.* New York: Little & Co., 1886, pp. 91-101. Discusses the importance of psychology for teachers. Criticizes the concept of learning by doing because it does not "give any hint as to what we should learn to do." Refers to the work of

Friedrich Diesterweg who was an advocate of self-activity in "service of the truth, beauty, and good." Stating that it is not what the teacher does, but what the teacher gets the pupils to do, that is of value. Describes how to fulfill Diesterweg's advice by listing suggestions. Describes physiological psychology, stages of thinking, arrested development, and how to move to the highest stage of thinking.

184. "Kindergarten Methods Contrasted with the Methods of the American Primary School." *National Education Association Journal of Proceedings and Addresses, 1889.* Topeka: Kansas Publishing House, 1889, pp. 448-453. Presents a lengthy discussion of the differences between the kindergarten curriculum and methods for children ages 4 through 6 and the curriculum and methods in primary school for ages 7 through 12. States that the primary school should not change its methods to incorporate kindergarten games, gifts, and occupations, citing the differences in the needs of the two age groups. Describes language development and the need for primary age students to work rather than play. States that in the primary school the conventional takes the place of the symbolic.

185. "The Kindergarten in the Public School System." In *Kindergarten and Child Culture Papers on Froebel's Kindergarten with Suggestions on Principles and Methods of Child Culture in Different Countries.* Republished from the *American Journal of Education,* ed. Henry Barnard. Hartford: Office of Barnard's *American Journal of Education,* 1890, pp. 625-642. Describes the advantages to the community and to the children of making the kindergarten part of the public schools. Discusses the problems of urban poverty and describes the kindergarten work in St. Louis in each essential area of development for young children, citing habits of cleanliness, preparation for trades, self-control, the ability to work with others, and preparation for work in primary and upper grades.

186. "How Imitation Grows into Originality and Freedom." *Kindergarten Magazine* 11 (May 1899): 600-601: From a lecture at the Kindergarten College, Chicago, April 1899. Describes how a child moves from imitation as copying to spontaneous activity as imitation becomes internalized and the child begins to connect the purposes and motives for actions. Cautions that once the leap is made the child should not be held back by kindergarten symbolic activities, but must be sent to the primary school where he/she can work rather than play. Also states that teachers should not push children away from the symbolic stage too soon.

187. "Kindergarten Psychology. Four Abstracts of Lectures Delivered at the Kindergarten College, Chicago, Illinois, April 1899 by William T. Harris." *School and Home Education* (April 1899): 3-30. (1) "Two Kinds of Psychology" describes psychology as important in helping the teacher diagnose the child's method of thinking and observation and which of three stages of thought the child thinks in. Describes rational psychology as a study of the development of the mind and empirical or scientific psychology as the study of the body and its help or hindrance of the growth of the

mind. States that a school psychology needs to include information from both rational and empirical psychology. Arrested development is the most important psychological area of study for educators and both types of psychology are needed to study this problem. (2) "How Symbolic Thinking Grows into Logical Thinking" describes the process by which children learn to move from symbolic thought in early childhood to logical thought by understanding the sequential steps involved in the production of a real object or the "chain of causality." (3) "How Imitation Becomes Originality" describes how children move from imitation to spontaneous action and show interest in discovering the properties and qualities of things. When children make this move they are ready for the work in the primary grades. (4) "How to Educate the Feelings and Emotions through the Intellect and Will" discusses affective education or the development of feelings and character education. States that character education is education of the intellect for a world view and the education of the will is important for correct habit formation.

188. "The Future of the Kindergarten." *Publication Information Unknown. A copy of this Pamphlet is available at the Concord Free Public Library, Concord, Massachusetts.* Discusses the importance of the kindergarten as a link that helps the child make the transition between home and school. Criticizes Hall's assumption about the reasons for games and play in the kindergarten. Harris states that there must be a connection between play and school work and play should be connected to the development of the mind, the body, the senses, and moral responsibility. The kindergarten has a future for growth and influence if it does not overemphasize any one aspect of play or Froebel's Occupations because that will arrest future development. A balance in the kindergarten program is needed.

189. "The Kindergarten as a Preparation for the Highest Civilization." *School and Home Education* (May 1903): 3-24; *Atlantic Educational Journal* 6 (July-August 1903): 35-36. Describes the benefits of the kindergarten as the best system for the transition from the family to full-fledged school because the child from ages 4 to 6 has not yet hardened himself/herself through the influence of the slum or through the over indulgence of a rich family "so as to be beyond the help of a cure through school." The kindergarten is the best means to overcome the influence of urban slums and all cities, as a matter of self preservation, should organize a strong force of kindergartens. "Viewed in this special function of usefulness Froebel's kindergarten is a great blessing to civilization."

SECONDARY SOURCES—HARRIS

190. Blow, Susan Elizabeth. "In Memoriam: William Torrey Harris." *Kindergarten Magazine* 20 (December 1909): 259-261. A memorial tribute to Harris and his contribution to the kindergarten movement by his closest colleague.

191. Blow, Susan Elizabeth. "The Service of Dr. William T. Harris to the Kinder-garten." *Proceedings of the Seventeenth Annual Meeting of the International Kindergarten Union,* St. Louis, Missouri, April 27-29, 1910. Woburn, Massachusetts: Andrews Publishing Co., 1910, pp. 123-143. A personal tribute to Harris and his work in establishing kindergartens in the public schools of St. Louis.

192. Cremin, Lawrence A. *American Education. The Metropolitan Experience 1876-1980.* New York: Harper & Row, 1988, pp. 157-165. Analysis of Harris' contributions to education and educational philosophy. The bib-liographic essay discusses the best sources about Harris' life and work.

193. Curti, Merle. *The Social Ideas of American Educators with a New Chapter on the Last Twenty-Five Years.* New Jersey: Littlefield, Adams & Co., 1965, pp. 310-347. An analysis of Harris' work in education, calling him "a representative social philosopher." States that his influence may be "related to the skill and plausibility with which Harris told two genera-tions of Americans what they already believed."

194. Evans, Henry Ridgely. "A List of the Writings of William Torrey Harris." *The Report of the Commissioner of Education for 1907.* Washington D.C.: Government Printing Office, 1908, pp. 37-72. A chronological bibliogra-phy with a subject index of Harris' works from 1866-1908.

195. Holmes, Brian. "Some Writings of William Torrey Harris." *British Journal of Educational Studies* 5 (1956-1957): 47-66. Provides an analysis of Harris' philosophy of education and his contributions in relation to other prominent educators of the time, such as John Dewey, Horace Mann, Henry Barnard, and others. Describes Harris' views on the kindergarten, the fam-ily, minority education, and vocational education stating that Dewey's approach was American while Harris' was typically European. States that "Dewey was able to reconcile tradition and future progress by accepting change while maintaining that it should and could be controlled through intellectual human activity. Harris certainly did not deny change, but could not whole heartedly accept it or at least not change which moved beyond the boundaries placed around it by Hegel."

196. Leidecker, Kurt F. *Bibliography: William Torrey Harris in Literature.* Co-lumbia, Missouri: University of Missouri, n. d. Provides a list of sources about Harris.

197. Leidecker, Kurt F. *Yankee Teacher: The Life of William Torrey Harris.* New York: Philosophical Library, 1946. A biography presenting Harris' life and career. Highlights Harris' work as Superintendent of Schools in St. Louis and as U. S. Commissioner of Education. Provides endnotes with much of Harris' correspondence. Still the most comprehensive biography of Harris.

198. McCluskey, Neil Gerard. *Public Schools and Moral Education: The Influ-ence of Horace Mann, William Torrey Harris, and John Dewey.* New York: Columbia University Press, 1958, pp. 99-176. Discusses Harris' career in

New England and St. Louis, and his tenure as U.S. Commissioner of Education providing biographical information. Analyzes Harris' contributions to philosophy and education stating that there is a striking similarity between Harris and Horace Mann. Provides an extensive bibliography of primary sources in chronological order.

199. Niel, Harriet. "William Torrey Harris." In *Pioneers of the Kindergarten in America. Prepared by the Committee of Nineteen, the International Kindergarten Union.* New York: The Century Company, 1924, pp. 167-183. A memoir of Harris' life and work in the kindergarten movement with emphasis on his role in establishing kindergartens in the St. Louis Public Schools. No footnotes or bibliography provided.

200. Shapiro, Michael Steven. *Children's Garden. The Kindergarten Movement from Froebel to Dewey.* University Park: The Pennsylvania State University, 1983, pp. 45-63. Discusses the kindergarten movement in St. Louis, Susan Blow's work with Harris, and provides a detailed view of Harris' educational reforms in the St. Louis Public Schools. Provides extensive endnotes. Also provides information on Harris' life and work with the Hegelian Society. States that when Harris left St. Louis in 1880 the kindergarten experiment declined and collapsed in 1884 because Harris was not onsite to supervise.

201. Troen, Selwyn K. *The Public and the Schools. Shaping the St. Louis System, 1838-1929.* Columbia: University of Missouri Press, 1975, pp. 99-115. Discusses the efforts of Harris and Blow to establish kindergartens in the St. Louis Public Schools. Provides insight into Harris' desire for urban social reform through the kindergarten. Extensive footnotes and bibliographic note provide primary sources.

202. Vanderwalker, Nina C. *The Kindergarten in American Education.* New York: Macmillan, 1908; Arno Press & The New York Times, 1971, (repr.) pp. 20-23, 34, 78-79, 153, 185-186, 192, 194-196. Describes Harris' contributions to the kindergarten movement, stating that the experimental kindergarten classes in the St. Louis Public Schools did a great deal to make St. Louis a center for teacher training and to enlighten other superintendents about the value of the kindergarten.

203. Weber, Evelyn. *The Kindergarten: Its Encounter with Educational Thought in America.* New York: Teachers College Press, 1969, pp. 27-30, 34, 40, 50. Describes Harris' philosophy of education, stating that he saw the kindergarten as a way to salvage the pampered children of the rich, as a means to save the poor from the slums, as a preparation for industrial training through Froebel's Gifts and Occupations, and as a transition from home to school for children ages 3 through 7. Harris believed that kindergarten methods should not follow the child to primary grades where work should replace play as the method of instruction. Discusses Harris' work with Susan Blow in St. Louis and briefly his NEA work. Excellent bibliography of primary sources.

204. Wesley, Edgar B. *NEA: The First Hundred Years; The Building of the Teach-ing Profession.* New York: Harper & Brothers, 1957, pp. 14, 45, 48-49, 54, 67, 70, 108-109, 113, 120, 131, 158, 162, 167, 186-187, 189-191, 213, 219-223, 245-255, 257, 259, 261, 263, 265, 290, 295-296. Discusses Harris' contributions to education and his work within the NEA and in the kindergarten movement, describing the development of teacher training classes in St. Louis. States that Harris was part of the 1872 NEA commit-tee chaired by William Hailmann which explored Froebel's kindergarten and its adaption to American education.

205. Wheelock, Lucy, Caroline D. Aborn, and Sarah A. Marble. *The History of the Kindergarten Movement in the Mid-Western States and New York.* Presented at the Cincinnati Convention of the Association for Childhood Education, April 19-23, 1938. Washington, D.C.: ACE, 1938, pp. 38-40. Describes the work of Harris and Blow as founders of the kindergarten in the St. Louis Public Schools. It states that "to Miss Susan Blow and Dr. William T. Harris honor and gratitude belong for one of the greatest achievements in the history of the St. Louis Public Schools."

PRIMARY SOURCES—BLOW

206. "The Mother Play and Nursery Songs." In *The Kindergarten and Child Cul-ture Papers on Froebel's Kindergarten with Suggestions on Principles and Methods of Child Culture in Different Countries,* ed. Henry Barnard. Hartford: Office of *Barnard's American Journal of Education,* 1890, pp. 575-594. Discusses Froebel's original songs and games and provides an introductory discussion of Froebel's philosophy. Analyses of specific songs and mottoes describes their significance for children's growth and devel-opment.

207. "Some Aspects of the Kindergarten." In *The Kindergarten and Child Cul-ture Papers on Froebel's Kindergarten with Suggestions on Principles and Methods of Child Culture in Different Countries,* ed. Henry Barnard. Hartford: Office of Barnard's *American Journal of Education,* 1890, pp. 595-616. Discusses the kindergarten program and activities with refer-ences to Froebel's philosophy and its interpretation.

208. *Symbolic Education, A Commentary on Froebel's Mother Play.* New York: D. Appleton, 1894. This is a less practical, more theoretical discussion of Froebel's original songs and games.

209. *Mottoes and Commentaries of Friedrich Froebel's Mother Play.* New York: D. Appleton, 1895. Provides a discussion of Froebel's philosophy and teaching ideas along with translations of the original songs and games by Blow and other kindergarten teachers, students, writers, and musicians.

210. *Letters to a Mother on the Philosophy of Froebel.* New York: D. Appleton, 1899. A collection of translations of Froebel's original songs and games for children, materials to use with children, and a children's book intended

for parents. Much of Blow's writing deals with the Mother Play through songs and games because she believed that these materials were more important than the Gifts and Occupations.

211. *Educational Issues in the Kindergarten.* New York: D. Appleton, 1908. Discusses the controversial issues causing division among kindergarten educators, such as free play, the methods of using literature, Herbartianism, socialization, and industrialization of education.

212. "First Report." In *The Kindergarten: Reports of the Committee of Nineteen on the Theory and Practice of the Kindergarten.* Authorized by the International Kindergarten Union. London: George G. Harp & Co., 1913; Boston: Houghton and Co., printed simultaneously 1913, pp. 1-230. The report is presented in four parts: Parts 1 through 3 are a theoretical interpretation of Froebel's philosophy of the kindergarten. Part 4 is a detailed discussion of a kindergarten program based on the first three parts of the report.

SECONDARY SOURCES—BLOW

213. "A Great St. Louis Woman." *St. Louis Globe Democrat,* March 28, 1916, p. 10. A discussion of Blow's contributions to the education of children in St. Louis. This is an obituary tribute.

214. Fisher, Laura. "Susan Elizabeth Blow." In *Pioneers of the Kindergarten in America.* Prepared by the Committee of Nineteen. New York: The Century Co., 1924, pp. 184-203. A discussion of Blow's life, her contributions to the establishment of public kindergartens in St. Louis, her work in the International Kindergarten Union, and her lectures defending the Froebelian point of view at Teachers College, Columbia University.

215. Johnston, Bertha. "Miss Blow's Chicago Lecture." *Kindergarten Magazine* (January 1906): 601-609. Summary and discussion of Blow's four lectures for the Chicago Kindergarten College given in May, 1905. States that Blow's lectures contained material from her publications, Harris' work, and Froebel's original writings.

216. Kirk, Lizzie Lee. *A Bibliography of Material By and About Susan Elizabeth Blow: A Study Presented to the Examination Committee of the St. Louis Public Library in Fulfillment of the Requirement for Promotion to Grade 11.* December, 1961, St. Louis, Missouri. An extensive bibliography of primary and secondary sources available in the St. Louis Public Library. Can be requested from the main library. A starting point for research on Blow and her contributions to early childhood education.

217. "Susan E. Blow: Founder of City Kindergarten, Succumbs in New York." *St. Louis Star-Times,* March 27, 1916. An obituary providing a discussion of Blow's life and career.

218. "Susan E. Blow Passes." *New York Times,* March 29, 1916, p. 11, col. 5. An obituary discussing Blow's contributions to education.

219. Thrusfield, Richard E. *Henry Barnard's American Journal of Education.* Baltimore: John Hopkins Press, 1945, pp. 283-284. A brief discussion of Blow's work in the kindergarten movement.

220. Troen, Selwyn K. *The Public and the Schools: Shaping the St. Louis System, 1838-1920.* Columbia: University of Missouri Press, 1975, pp. 2, 10, 99, 103-104. Presents brief information about Blow's life and work, with emphasis on her connection with William Torrey Harris in establishing kindergartens and training kindergarten teachers in St. Louis.

Elizabeth Harrison (1849-1927)

Founder of the National College of Education, Harrison demanded high standards for admission and training from those who wished to teach young children.

Harrison studed with Alice Putnam, Susan Blow, Maria Kraus-Boelte, Baroness Bertha von Marenholtz-Bulow, and Maria Montessori. She founded the Chicago Kindergarten Club with Alice Putnam; lectured nationally to mothers with Mrs. John N. Crouse; established the Chicago Kindergarten Training School (1887), which became the Chicago Kindergarten College, with a three-year training program; as well as the National Kindergarten College (1912), the National Kindergarten and Elementary College (1917), and the National College of Education (1930). Only high school graduates were admitted to these training schools, which provided a three-year (and later a four-year) bachelor's degree program that included humanities, sciences, social sciences, and pedagogical studies. Harrison was a lecturer, author, and parents advocate; a member of the International Kindergarten Union Advisory Committee (1892-1910), Parents Committee (1902-1907), Teacher Training Committee (1902, 1909-1916), and Committee of 15 (1902-1929), which became the Committee of 19. She was a member of the American Child Welfare Association, National Board of the Congress of Mothers and a leader of the Conservative-Liberal Subcommittee of the Committee of 19. She believed in a combination of Froebel's philosophy and a scientific approach to the kindergarten, and was unable to decide which committee to join when the Conservative-Liberal split; she joined both.

Harrison worked to teach parents and teachers the value of creative arts in child development and founded a teacher training program that became a model for the profession.

PRIMARY SOURCES

221. *A List of Books for Children Recommended from the Kindergarten Standpoint.* Pamphlet, 1889. Consists of five lists of recommended books: (1) nine books to read to children, (2) thirty-seven to read with children, (3) fifteen for children in science, (4) sixteen for teachers and mothers to read dealing with child study and child development such as *Émile* by Rousseau and *Leonard and Gertrude* by Pestalozzi, and (5) nineteen books for teachers and mothers on science.

222. *A Study of Child Nature: From the Kindergarten Standpoint.* Chicago: Chicago Kindergarten College, 1890. Presents Harrison's lectures in three categories: the body, the mind, and the soul, describing instincts and their training in the three categories. The Body discusses training the muscles,

senses, emotions, and affection. The Mind discusses the training of reason, the instinct of right and wrong, the instinct of recognition and training the will. The Soul discusses instincts of reverence or the training of
worship, and the instinct of imitation or the training of faith. A popular
book translated into eight languages, it had gone through 50 editions by
1942. A series of questions were published to accompany the book at the
request of the Woman's Council and Mother's Circle of Akron, Ohio, in
1897. In 1915 Dr. L.W. Sackett of the University of Texas published a
second set of questions used by Parent-Teachers Associations as a study
guide to Harrison's book.

223. *In Story-Land.* Chicago: Central Publishing, 1895. Myths for children, which
were essentially sermons.

224. *Two Children of the Foothills.* Chicago: Sigma Publishing, 1900. The daily
lives of a boy and girl growing up in the Sierra Madre Mountains of California, showing the use of kindergarten theory and practice for mothers.
Provided an application of kindergarten methods to child care at home.
Written after she had had a rest cure in the area.

225. *Misunderstood Children; Sketches Taken from Life.* Chicago: Central Publishing, 1910. Describes undesirable behavior and ways to correct it. Uses
psychological principles to understand heredity and environment, the effects of body conditions on mental conditions, the effects of mind on the
body, and the bad effects of too much freedom or too much authoritarian
control. Describes how neglect of these ideas causes problems and provides suggestions for improving behavior, often citing common-sense
solutions.

226. *The Kindergarten: Report of the Committee of Nineteen on the Theory and
Practice of the Kindergarten.* London George G. Harp & Co., 1913; Boston: Houghton-Mifflin, 1913; pp. 297-301. Presents the report of the Lib-
eral-Conservative committee that discussed the need for change based on
psychological research and asked kindergartners to adjust their work to
comply with that of the primary grades to make the kindergarten part of
an "organized whole." This is the shortest of the reports and very well
presented.

227. *The Montessori Method and the Kindergarten.* United States Bureau of Education Bulletin No. 28. Washington, D.C.: Government Printing Office,
1914. Commissioned by the International Kindergarten Union in 1912,
Harrison wrote the report after a five month visit to Montessori's school
in Italy. Provides a list of four limitations of the Montessori Method: over-
emphasis on individual rather than group development; omission of stories from the curriculum; no materials for self-expression; and no definite
position on religious training. Praises Montessori for a valuable contribution to understanding young children through child study.

228. "The Growth of the Kindergarten in the United States." In *Pioneers of the
Kindergarten in America,* eds. Caroline D. Aborn, Catherine Watkins,
and Lucy Wheelock. Prepared by the Committee of Nineteen. New York:

Century Company, 1924, pp. 3-16. Part I presents a brief discussion of Froebel as a child and the influence of his early life on the development of the kindergarten. Part II gives a chronology of the kindergarten in America and a review of the people who helped the idea grow. States that the changes in methods in American schools can be in part traced to the influence of Froebel's work.

229. *Sketches Along Life's Road,* ed. C.S. Bailey. Boston: Stanford, 1930. Autobiographical account of Harrison's work in the Kindergarten Movement, edited and published after her death. Firsthand view of the people and events that shaped the beginning of early childhood education.

SECONDARY SOURCES

230. Branch, Sandra Faye. *Elizabeth Harrison and Her Contribution to the Kindergarten Movement in Chicago 1880-1920.* Ph.D. diss. Loyola University, Chicago, 1992. Good bibliography of primary sources. Provides a biography and analysis of Harrison's work along with a chronology of the history of the Kindergarten Movement. The only bibliography of Harrison's writings available.

231. "Elizabeth Harrison Memorial Tribute." CHAFF. Chicago: National College of Education, 1927, 5, 3, 1-3. A tribute to the founder of the National College of Education at the time of her death.

232. Marshall, Helen. "Elizabeth Harrison Pioneer Woman Teacher." *Delta Kappa Gamma Bulletin* 8, (June 1942): 9-10. Presents a brief biographical sketch and discusses Harrison's work.

233. "Miss Harrison and the Chicago Kindergarten College." *Kindergarten Magazine* 5 (June 1893): 739-745. Provides biographical information and discusses the training school Harrison founded. Provides insight into the way the training school was viewed and presented to those who might consider attending it.

234. Snyder, Agnes. *Dauntless Women in Childhood Education, 1865-1931.* Washington, D.C.: Association for Childhood Education International, 1972, pp. 127-163. Provides biographical information, references to primary sources, and a picture of Harrison. Good starting point for research on Harrison.

Patty Smith Hill (1868-1946)

The unification and restructuring of kindergarten and primary education was the aim of Hill's work.

Hill's successes in early childhood education include the unification of the kindergarten and first grade so that one teacher could work with both the kindergarten and primary grades; a revision of the curriculum to include new songs, equipment, and activities to promote creativity, social living, and better meet the needs of young children; more work with parents; and changes in teacher training to include theory based on the work's of John Dewey, Edward L. Thorndike, Granville Stanley Hall, and William H. Kilpatrick. She encouraged the spread of nursery schools and was a leader in the International Kindergarten Union and the Committee of Nineteen, as well as the Speyer and Horace Mann schools which served as models for training teachers and innovations. Hill supported the link between Teachers' College, Columbia University and model schools to validate the professional status of early childhood educators. She developed large wooden floor blocks called Hill blocks.

Under Hill's leadership early childhood education moved away from Friedrich Froebel's idealism toward a modern scientific knowledge base.

PRIMARY SOURCES

235. and Mildred J. Hill. *Song Stories for the Kindergarten.* Chicago: Clayton E. Summy & Co., 1896. Words by Patty Smith Hill and music by Mildred J. Hill. The collection includes "Good Morning to You" and "Happy Birthday."

236. "Free Play." *Proceeding of the Seventh Annual Meeting of the International Kindergarten Union,* April 18-20, 1900. Brooklyn, New York. Chicago: Donnelley & Sons Printers, 1900, pp. 108-113. Discusses the function of free play and games and their place in the kindergarten curriculum; the advantages and disadvantages of substituting traditional games for kindergarten games, and concludes that it would be as much of a mistake to disregard traditional games as it would be to substitute them for kindergarten games.

237. "Some Conservative and Progressive Phases of Kindergarten Education." *The Sixth Yearbook of the National Society for the Study of Education. Part II the Kindergarten and Its Relation to Elementary Education,* ed. Manfred, J. Holmes. Chicago: Public School Publishing Co., 1907, pp. 61-85. Discusses the conditions and causes that gave rise to the reactionary movement; the present status of the Conservative and Progressive

movements; the fundamental theoretical points at issue; the points of difference in practice between the conservative and reactionary movements;
and the present and future needs of the kindergarten. Concludes with a
discussion on the importance of a combination of kindergarten and primary education.

238. "Some Hopes and Fears for the Kindergarten of the Future." *Proceeding of
the Twentieth Annual Meeting of the International Kindergarten Union,*
April 29-May 2, 1913, Washington, D.C. Cleveland, Ohio: A.S. Gilman
Printing Co., 1913, pp. 89-101. Discusses the three major issues in the
history of the kindergarten, describing the five problems that need to be
solved by modifications in teacher training and practice. Concludes that
education must allow the young in the profession the opportunity to try
new ideas.

239. "Second Report." In *The Kindergarten: Reports of the Committee of Nine-
teen on the Theory and Practice of the Kindergarten.* Authorized by the
International Kindergarten Union. London: George G. Harp & Co., 1913;
Boston: Houghton-Mifflin, 1913, pp. 231-294. Presents the break with
Froebelianism and the development of modern early childhood education
based on the work, of John Dewey, Granville Stanley Hall, and Edward L.
Thorndike. Discusses the principles and practices of selecting and orga-
nizing subject matter drawing on Dewey's *My Pedagogic Creed,* and *The
Child and the Curriculum,* and William James' *Psychology* and *Talks to
Teachers.* Describes practice based on this theory and a selection of mate-
rials as well as methods of conducting training classes.

240. "The Project, An Adaption of a Life Method of Thought and Action." *Proceedings of the Twenty-eighth Annual Meeting of the International Kindergarten Union,* May 2-6, 1921, Detroit, Michigan. Rochester, New York:
Andrews Publishing Co., 1921, pp. 153-155. Describes the origins of the
Project Method and the advantages of the approach; provides a list of the
development of projects for different ages; and describes materials and
suggestions for teachers. Concludes that the Project Method is the best
suited to "character development, morality, and social training."

241. "Introduction." In *A Conduct Curriculum for Kindergarten and First Grade,*
by Agnes Burke, Edith U. Conard, Alice Dalgleish, Edna V. Hughes, Mary
E. Rankin, and Charlotte G. Garrison. New York: Scribners, 1923. Discusses the necessity for the unification of the kindergarten and the first
grade. Provides the background for the five-year study of the application
of Thorndike's principles of learning to the kindergarten reported in the
book. Those involved in the study advocated a free social organization in
the classroom to help children develop social behaviors necessary for later
life.

242. "Changes in Curricula and Methods in Kindergarten Education." *Childhood
Education* 2 (November 1925): 99-106. Discusses the reasons for the slow
response of the kindergarten to the scientific movement in education. De-

scribes the contributions of John Dewey, G. Stanley Hall, and Arnold Gesell to a better understanding of children and their needs as the basis for the early childhood curriculum. Concludes that changes in children's habits and attitudes for the better will come about when home and school work together to build a curriculum to make the learning process continuous.

243. "Department of Nursery Education: The Education of the Nursery School Teacher." *Childhood Education* 3 (October, 1926): 72-80. A systematic discussion of the education of the nursery school teacher and the need to organize a training curriculum. Suggests the use of a daily record of observation of individual children to develop a scientific base of analytic data on growth and development that would describe the physical, intellectual, emotional, and social growth of each child. Provides an excerpt from an experienced teacher's daily record.

244. "First Steps in Character Education." *Childhood Education* 3 (April 1927): 355-359. Discusses the place of character education in early childhood curriculum and asks: What enters into character education? When does character begin? How permanent is early training? Discusses the beginning of habit and character in early life and concludes that scientific data cannot be ignored and must be applied to the preschool years to provide children with the right start in character education.

245. "The Strategic Position of the Kindergarten in American Education." *Childhood Education* 6 (December 1929): 147-152. Discusses the position of the kindergarten in the educational system, raising numerous questions about the value and importance of early learning. Makes a good case for early intervention programs such as Head Start, which were put into effect 60 years after the article was written.

SECONDARY SOURCES

246. Jammer, M. Charlotte. *Patty Smith Hill and Reform of the American Kindergarten.* Ph.D. diss. Teachers College, Columbia University, 1960. Analysis of Hill's work and educational philosophy. Provides a history of the Kindergarten Movement with a discussion of the key figures involved. Extensive bibliography of primary and secondary sources.

247. "Patty Smith Hill." *New York Times,* May 26, 1946, p. 32. Obituary discussing Hill's life and work in early childhood education.

248. Rasmussen, Margaret. "Over the Editor's Desk." *Childhood Education* 37 (March 1961): 7. Recollections by Rasmussen of Hill discussing the impact of her work. Rasmussen states that she heard Hill speak after her retirement from Teachers College and very few people came to the lecture, but "what she taught was never to be forgotten."

249. Snyder, Agnes. *Dauntless Women in Childhood Education 1856-1931.* Washington, D.C.: Association for Childhood Education International, 1972, pp. 233-280. A discussion of Hill's life and work highlighting her work

for kindergarten reform. No bibliography is provided but footnotes are complete.

Amy M. Hostler (1898-1987)

Memories of her own kindergarten experience motivated Hostler to become a teacher, but study with Alice Temple convinced her of the importance of the early childhood years.

Hostler was the director of the Western Reserve University day care center and nursery school; Executive Secretary of the National Federation of Day Nurseries; and trained the first nursery school and kindergarten teachers in Puerto Rico, where she helped establish public kindergartens and earned the title "Mother of Puerto Rican Kindergartens." She also held positions as the director of New York City Works Project Administration nurseries and regional consultant to the W.P.A. on nursery schools in the Southern states; dean of Mills School for Kindergarten Teachers and first president of Mills College of Education; president of the National Association for Nursery Education, now known as National Association for the Education of Young Children; vice-president of the Association for Childhood Education representing nursery school education; and chairperson of the Teacher Training Committee, member of the publications committee, co-chairperson New York City local study conference, and financial consultant all for the Association for Childhood Education International. She authored numerous articles for parents and teachers; was president of the U.S. National Committee of the World Organization for Early Childhood Education, and vice-president for Brazil, Canada, and America; and, after retirement, worked with the Arizona State Legislature and Arizona State University.

Hostler inspired future teachers, worked for international early childhood educational standards, and helped build the foundation for quality day care programs.

PRIMARY SOURCES

250. and Gertrude Bicknell. "Science Experiences in the Nursery School." *Childhood Education* 8, no. 7 (March 1932): 342-348. Describes science activities for 2 to 3½ year olds and 3½ to 5 year olds at Western Reserve University under the guidance of Bicknell, who had majored in biology. Describes in detail the aims of instruction for both groups and highlights instructional activities and the background and needs of the children.

251. "Establishing Nursery Schools in Puerto Rico." *Childhood Education* 11, no. 3 (December 1934): 131-132. Describes the establishment of nursery schools on Puerto Rico including details such as scheduling, materials, activities, and teacher training. The United States office of Education and the University of Puerto Rico sponsored the training which Hostler and Emma Harris taught. The course was titled the Emergency Nursery School

Course and the first 156 young women admitted helped staff 50 nursery schools. Hostler and Harris also toured the island scouting sites for nursery schools. The article describes the training that was established by Hostler and replicated by others and earned Hostler the title "Mother of Puerto Rican Kindergartens."

252. "Some Get Along, Some Don't. Why?" *National Parent Teacher* 49 (October 1954): 21-23. Discusses children's adjustment to school and the reasons why some children have problems either with other children or with other factors such as curriculum.

253. "Standards for Teachers in Early Childhood Education. A Statement by the ACEI Teacher Education Committee. Amy M. Hostler Chairman." *Childhood Education* 35, no. 2 (October 1958): 65-66. A preliminary statement regarding the requirements for professional advancement and training for Early Childhood teachers. Discusses course content for training and describes the need for periodic refresher courses or workshops and organizational membership as a means for keeping abreast of current research and its application to classroom practice.

SECONDARY SOURCES

254. "Amy M. Hostler." *ACEI Exchange* (May, 1988): 3. An obituary describing Hostler's life and contributions to education. Highlights her work in Puerto Rico, her Presidency of Mills College of Education, and her work in New York City as director of 16 W.P.A. nurseries.

255. Meyer, Alberta L. "Amy M. Hostler. Mother of Puerto Rican Kindergartens." *Childhood Education* 68, no. 4 (Summer 1992): 239, 242-244. Reprinted in *Profiles in Childhood Education* 1931-1960, ed. ACEI Later Leaders Committee. Washington, D.C.: Association for Childhood Education International, 1992, pp. 14-18. Presents a biography of Hostler and discusses her early life; her education and training as a teacher; her work in early childhood education; her achievements, such as the presidency of Mills College of Education and the establishment of kindergartens in Puerto Rico; and her international work for the World Organization for Early Childhood Education-Organisation Mondial pour l'Éducation Préscolaire. It concludes with her work in Arizona after retirement from Mills College of Education. Hostler became an advocate for children at Arizona State University, Tempe and in the Arizona State Legislature.

Leland B. Jacobs (1907-1992)

Children are our future, Jacobs stated, in the 1986 keynote address at the Association for Childhood Education International's Annual Conference, and deserve "a genuine cultural investment" by educators to ensure that their rights "to be playful, to wonder, and to construct and...reconstruct knowledge" are protected.

Jacobs contributed more than forty story and poetry books for children; taught training programs for teachers in literature, language arts, and early childhood curriculum at Ohio State University and Teachers College, Columbia University; and held a lifetime membership in the Association for Childhood Education International. He was the author of numerous journal articles and books, including a long-running column in *Teaching Pre K-8* and *Using Literature with Young Children;* an international lecturer and consultant; and a founding member of the International Reading Association, the National Conference on Research in English, the National Council of Teachers of English, and the Association for Childhood Education International. Jacobs worked with the New Jersey Reading Association; was elected to the Reading Hall of Fame; received the Distinguished Teacher Award from Mills College of Education; and was commited to the development of young minds through literature and stories.

Jacobs believed that educators must support the "lonely real teachers" in their efforts on the behalf of young children.

PRIMARY SOURCES

256. Herrick, Vergil E. and Jacobs, Leland B., eds. *Children and the Language Arts.* New Jersey: Prentice-Hall, 1955. A text containing chapters on the language arts written by nineteen authorities in the field. Each contributor discusses his or her area of expertise. Jacobs writes on "Children's Experiences in Literature," which describes methods and materials that provide good experiences with literature for children in all grades.
257. *Using Literature with Young Children.* New York: Teachers College Press, 1965. Presents twelve strategies for teaching literature to young children.
258. "Science Fiction for Children." *Instructor Magazine* 79, no. 5 (November 1970): 71-72. Describes methods for teaching science fiction books and suggests several books to use.
259. "Humanism in Teaching Reading." *Phi Delta Kappan,* 52, no. 8 (March 1971): 464-467. States that the reading program should emphasize the affective development of children, not just the development of skills. Describes the emotional and affective elements in reading instruction.

260. "The Meaning of Teaching." *Childhood Education* 54, no. 6 (April 1978): 280-286. Describes three kinds of teachers and states that teaching as an art requires recognition of children's interests helping them to learn concepts and aesthetic feelings.
261. "Inside Information: Guidelines for Choosing Informational Trade Books." *Teaching PRE K-8* 8, no. 21 (October 1990): 106-107. Jacobs provides suggestions for selecting information or nonfiction books for children.
262. "What is Teaching?" *Teaching PRE K-8* 8, no. 21 (May 1991): 122-123. Discusses teaching from several perspectives to describe successful strategies with children.
263. "Biographical Notes." *Teaching PRE K-8* 8, no. 22 (February 1992): 95-97. Suggestions for using biography with all curriculum areas.

SECONDARY SOURCES

264. Bergen, Doris. "Leland B. Jacobs: Fostering the Authority of Children." *Childhood Education* 69, no. 1 (Fall 1992): 33-35. A profile of Jacobs discussing his work in children's literature as an author of books and poems for children, and as an advocate for children's literature that meets the needs of its audience.
265. "Dr. Leland Jacobs, 85, Educator and Columbia Professor Emeritus." *New York Times,* April 7, 1992, B.7. An obituary with photograph discussing Jacobs' life and work.
266. "Leland Blair Jacobs (1907-1992)," *School Library Journal* 38 (May 1992): 12. An obituary discussing Jacobs' career as author and advocate of children's literature.
267. "Poet in the Classroom: *Teaching* Watches Leland B. Jacobs in Action and Learns How a Poetry Lesson Should Be Taught." *Teaching PRE K-8* 8, no. 20 (April 1990): 39-40. Provides an illustrated discussion of Jacobs' poetry lesson for an elementary school class.

William Heard Kilpatrick (1871-1965)

Called "the million dollar professor" because of the thousands of students he attracted to Teachers College, Columbia University, Kilpatrick was considered to be the most influential force in teacher training of the twentieth century.

Kilpatrick's contributions to early childhood education include the development of the Project Method, which changed curriculum and classroom activities by providing teachers with clean guidelines for organizing and structuring the school day. The Project Method helped early childhood teachers to structure the curriculum into units which helped them organize each subject around a central theme with appropriate child centered activities. He interpreted John Dewey's ideas for classroom teachers; authored numerous articles and books, including *Foundations of Method* and *Education for a Changing Civilization;* and advocated using pupil's developmental needs, interests, and problem-solving skills as the basis for classroom activities. Kilpatrick tried to reshape the role of the teacher from an authoritarian figure to that of a guide and worked for changes in teacher preparation programs. He was also a member of the Association for Childhood Education International advisory and editorial boards.

Kilpatrick's work changed the classroom from teacher-centered to child-centered and restructured the kindergarten-primary curriculum to allow subject matter to be organized in innovative ways.

PRIMARY SOURCES

268. "Montessori and Froebel." *Kindergarten Review* 23 (April 1913): 491-496.
Kilpatrick examines and compares the work of Freidrich Froebel and Maria Montessori describing the attitude of Froebel and Montessori toward a scientific study of education; the doctrine of liberty of the child and its doctrine of character development; the adequacy of self-expression in both systems; the doctrine of auto-education; the utilization of systematic training by means of material objectives; and preparation for the school arts, and the basic curriculum areas of reading, writing, and arithmetic. Concludes "that in terms of scientific attitude, individual liberty, and concrete life experiences the conservative kindergarten can learn from Montessori, however, in terms of materials, play, and social cooperation Montessori can learn from American methods....In America there is superior educational theory" which, if methods of early childhood education "were brought in line with the best that America otherwise knows, we should...need to hear but little of Froebel and less of Montessori."

269. *The Montessori System Examined.* Boston: Houghton-Mifflin, 1914; New York: Arno Press, 1971 (repr.). A critique of the Montessori methods which highlights its limitations written after a trip to Italy to observe the method. Kilpatrick's conclusion compares the Montessori Method to Dewey's work stating that Montessori indicates a "set of mechanically simple devices," but Dewey "could not secure the education which he sought in so simple a fashion." Provides an outline of the material discussed in each chapter. This critique is believed to be responsible for the decline of interest in the Montessori Method at the time of its publication.

270. *Froebel's Kindergarten Principles Critically Examined.* New York: Macmillan, 1916. An examination of Froebel's philosophy and methods. Examines the principles underlying Froebel's educational doctrines and psychology; the kindergarten Gifts and Occupations and additional elements of the kindergarten curriculum. Concludes that the kindergarten is an institution of possibilities and vision. Raises several questions: Will the kindergarten be able to rid itself of the old symbolism, fixed gifts, and prescribed program? Can the kindergarten lose its separate existence to merge with the elementary school? Also critiques the psychological deficiencies of Froebel's ideas.

271. "The Project Method." *Teachers College Record* 19 (September 1918): 319-335. Kilpatrick describes how to organize curriculum around a child's purposeful activities in a social environment. He outlines four kinds of projects that are useful in the kindergarten. They include: (1) Construction, for example, building a boat or participating in a play. (2) Appreciation of the aesthetic enjoyment, for example, listening to a story. (3) Problem solving, for example, finding out if dew falls. (4) Developing skill or knowledge in learning to write. Asserts that well organized projects involve motor activities in addition to cognitive and aesthetic experiences, and can help children learn attitudes, standards, and ideals that contribute to social learning which prepare children for later life. This article led kindergarten teachers to adopt new ideas about activities and materials and helped restructure the kindergarten curriculum.

272. "Introduction." In *An Experiment with a Project Curriculum,* by Ellsworth Collings. New York: Macmillan, 1923, pp. xvii-xxvi. Kilpatrick describes the underlying principles of Collings' experiment with the Project Method in a rural setting. He states that the book is a pioneering work of curriculum development, putting theory into practice, and evaluating and assessing outcomes.

273. "How Shall Early Education Conceive Its Objectives?" *Childhood Education* 2 (September 1925): 1-12. Written as a discussion among teachers the article describes the development of educational objective for the kindergarten. It concludes that developing a list of objectives to be taught would detract from "the educative experience and its reconstruction" because an ordered list of objectives would cause teachers to hunt for activi-

ties to fulfill the objectives and that educational objectives are of value only when used wisely.

274. *Foundations of Method: Informal Talks on Teaching.* New York: Macmillan, 1925. An elaboration of the Project Method proposing that a new education must not teach subjects separately, but must revolve around purposeful activities that go through four steps: purposing, planning, executing, and judging. The key element is that the plan and the purpose comes from the children and is not imposed by the teacher. Education must emphasize thinking skills and methods of problem solving. This proposal for a "new education" sounds very much like whole language, the integrated curriculum, and many other discoveries that all stem from Kilpatrick's work, Dewey's ideas, and the work of their students.

275. *Education for a Changing Civilization.* New York: Macmillan, 1926. States that education must prepare students for an uncertain future and should not limit them to the memorization of material. Educators must prepare students of every age to solve problems and think for themselves to become "self-reliant adaptable people...[to] face [a] changing world." This book influenced changes in the kindergarten and primary school curriculum because leaders in the Kindergarten Movement used the work of Progressives such as John Dewey and Kilpatrick to restructure kindergarten education.

SECONDARY SOURCES

276. Beck, Robert. "Kilpatrick's Critique of Montessori's Method and Theory." *Studies in Philosophy and Education* (November 1, 1961): 153-162. Describes Montessori's 1913 visit to America and the enthusiastic reception for her new education method. Also discusses the fears of many at Teachers College that the Montessori Method would take over the kindergarten. Kilpatrick went to Rome to observe the method first hand and his classic report was "the first book of genuinely critical examination," however, "he reported fairly." Describes the influence of Edward L. Thorndike and John Dewey in the critique. Concludes that after Kilpatrick's critique America and Europe never again enjoyed the closeness they had had before 1914 in sharing educational ideas. Kilpatrick became identified with the Progressive Movement after the critique was published and reviewed.

277. Campbell, David Norbert. *A Critical Analysis of William Heard Kilpatrick's The Montessori System Examined.* Ph. D. diss. University of Illinois at Urbana-Champaign, 1970. Discusses what happened prior to the 1914 publication of Kilpatrick's critique of Montessori. Examines Kilpatrick and the Montessori movement and Kilpatrick's specific charges against Montessori's psychology. Compares and contrast the general aspects of Kilpatrick's criticism with the prevailing doctrines of American education in 1914, and the decline in the Montessori movement. Evaluates the

Montessori system in the light of more recent discoveries and theories in preschool education; and concludes with remarks regarding Montessori education in America, both present and future. Provides a bibliography of primary and secondary sources.

278. Cremin, Lawrence A. *The Transformation of the Schools: Progressivism in American Education 1876-1957.* New York: Knopf, 1962, pp. 173, 215-219. Discusses Kilpatrick's philosophy and his role in Progressive educational reform.

279. "Memorial Issue on William Heard Kilpatrick." *Educational Theory* 16 (January 1966): 4-34,44-58,87-90. All of the articles in this issue are dedicated to Kilpatrick's life and career in education. Includes Samuel Tenenbaum "An Informal Essay on William Heard Kilpatrick and some of his Writings"; Isaac B. Berkson, F. Ernest Johnson,and Edward Lewis, "Statements Delivered at Memorial Service for William Kilpatrick"; William Van Til, "Introduction; On William Heard Kilpatrick"; and William W. Brickman, "William Heard Kilpatrick and International Education."

280. "Prof. Kilpatrick of Columbia Dies." *New York Times,* February 14, 1965, p. 92. Obituary discussing Kilpatrick's career at Teachers College, his three marriages, and the influence of the Project Method. Includes a photograph.

281. Swimmer, George Gershon. *A Comparison of the Intellectual Development of John Dewey and William Heard Kilpatrick with Implications for the Differences in Their Educational Theories.* Ph. D. diss., Northwestern University, 1957. Provides biographical information on Kilpatrick and Dewey, emphasizing their educational backgrounds and early teaching experiences, and compares the philosophies through their writings. Includes bibliography of primary and secondary sources.

282. Tenenbaum, Samuel. *William Heard Kilpatrick: Trail Blazer in Education.* New York: Harper, 1951. This biography of Kilpatrick presents an uncritical discussion of his life and work.

Lucy Craft Laney (1854-1933)

Founder of the Haines Normal and Industrial Institute, Laney set high academic standards by insisting on a liberal arts curriculum rather vocational training for her students.

Laney taught in the black public schools of Georgia; developed a program to educate nurses (which became the School of Nursing at Augusta University Hospital); developed a teacher education program; emphasized academic education for girls leading to college entrance; fought for the establishment of Georgia's first Black public high school; and established Augusta's first kindergarten in the early 1890s with contributions from the Lucy Laney League in New York. She was a member of the National Association of Colored Women, the Southeastern Federation of Women's Clubs, the Georgia State Teachers Association, the National YWCA, and served as chairperson of the Colored Section of the Interracial Commission of Augusta. In 1886, the year the Haines Institute was chartered by Georgia, she was the only Black woman administrator of a major school affiliated with the Presbyterian Church.

Laney was praised by President William Howard Taft for her tireless work in educating her students to reach their highest potential as human beings.

PRIMARY SOURCES

283. "A Progress Report From the Founder of the Haines School." *Church at Home and Abroad* (August 1893): 140. Describes visitors to the school, states that the reputation of the school was spreading, and reports the number of students enrolled. A brief account of the school seven years after its founding.

284. "The Burden of the Educated Colored Woman." A paper presented at the Hampton Negro Conference Number 3, July 1899. *Conference Proceedings Report,* pp. 37-42. Asserts that ignorance and its companions—shame, crime, and prejudice—are the burden of the educated Black woman. Discusses the need for education that stresses character and moral building by female teachers who are role models and the importance of hygiene and family structure. Posits that the burden's of ignorance, immorality, and prejudice can be lifted by culture, character, and money, and that this must be done through better homes, clean homes, better schools, and work. Places the responsibility on educated women to do this work to save the future because she feels women are the best teachers at all levels from kindergarten through college.

SECONDARY SOURCES

285. Brawley, Benjamin. *Negro Builders and Heroes.* Chapel Hill: University of
     North Carolina Press, 1937, pp. 279-282. Discusses Laney's life and work
     and includes a brief bibliography.
286. Daniel, Sadie Iola. *Women Builders.* Washington, D.C.: The Associated Pub-
     lishers, 1931. Revised and enlarged by Charles H. Wesley and Thelma D.
     Perry. Washington, D.C.: The Associate Publishers, 1969, pp. 1-27. The
     original volume contained seven biographies of African-American women
     who contributed to the education of young people. The revised edition
     added five more distinguished women. Photographs are included. There
     is no bibliography or footnotes, but Mary White Ovington's work is men-
     tioned in the Laney biography.
287. Dittmer, John, *Black Georgia in the Progressive Era 1900-1920.* Urbana:
     University of Illinois Press, 1977, pp. 149-151. Describes the Haines In-
     stitute as the best private school in Augusta. Presents a biography of Laney,
     with personal memories by her niece and pupils. Useful biographical notes
     and interesting sources.
288. Griggs, Augustus C. "Lucy Craft Laney." *Journal of Negro History* 19 (Janu-
     ary 1934): 97-102. A memorial tribute to Laney providing biographical
     material and a discussion of the impact of the work at the Haines Normal
     and Industrial Institute.
289. James, Edward T., Janet Wilson James, and Paul Boyer, eds. *Notable Ameri-
     can Women, 1607-1950.* Vol. 2. Cambridge: Harvard University Press,
     1971, pp. 365-367. Biography including Laney's early life, work as an
     educator, and school founder. Brief bibliography with incomplete cita-
     tions included.

John Locke (1632-1704)

Locke applied the scientific laws of his time to human development, believing that it proceeded according to specific laws. He believed that a person was not pre-formed at birth, but developed as a result of encounters with the environment.

Locke believed that the individual was a blank slate (*tabula rasa*) who received impressions from the environment via the senses, and that these impressions should be part of education. He placed strong emphasis on physical activity, believing in "a sound mind in a sound body," and felt that the family was responsible for education and so provided guidelines for parents. Locke conceived an educational model for the gentleman class who, he felt, needed physical toughness and mental sharpness.

Locke introduced America to the image of the English country gentleman whose strength came from wealth earned in commerce. He envisioned a government given power by the people who were granted protection of their natural rights to life, liberty, and property. Locke tried to understand the nature of people, to set educational goals for the good life, and to select the experiences necessary for achieving these goals.

PRIMARY SOURCES

290. *Some Thoughts Concerning Education.* London: Awnsham and John Churchill, 1693. Anonymous. *Some Thoughts Concerning Education.* Enlarged by Mr. John Locke. London: A. and J. Churchill, 1705. A series of letters written from Holland in 1684 to Edward Clarke giving advice on raising children. These letters provide a guide to raising a physically healthy young gentleman. The first two editions were published anonymously in 1693. The fifth edition published in 1705 is considered the definitive edition and Locke's name appears on the title page.

291. *Two Treatises on Government* Ed. by P. Laslett. Cambridge: Cambridge University Press. 1960. Locke's political theory, which denies the absolute rights of kings, was written while in exile in Holland in 1690.

SECONDARY SOURCES

292. Axtell, James L. *The Educational Writings of John Locke.* Cambridge: Cambridge University Press, 1968. Provides a detailed discussion of Locke's writings on education with an excellent checklist of publication dates from 1693-1966 in several languages and an extensive bibliography. The appendices provide the letters to Edward Clarke, a letter to Countess

Peterborough, and "Some Thoughts Concerning Reading and Study for a Gentleman 1703."

293. Cranston, Maurice. *John Locke: A Biography.* London: Longmans, 1957. A good biography discussing Locke's life from several perspectives, showing him as a correspondent, a traveler, and a busy person.

294. Gibson, James. *Locke's Theory of Knowledge and Its Historical Relations.* Cambridge: Cambridge University Press, 1917. Provides a detailed discussion of Locke's theory of knowledge with a section comparing his work with that of René Descartes, Gottfred Leibniz, and English philosophy.

295. Ulich, Robert. *History of Educational Thought* New York: American Book Co., 1968, pp. 200-210. Provides a clear discussion of Locke's educational philosophy with a bibliography.

296. Ulich, Robert. *Three Thousand Years of Educational Wisdom: Selections from Great Documents.* Cambridge: Harvard University Press, 1954, 1982 (revi.,) pp. 355-382. A brief discussion of Locke's life and work is followed by excerpts from *Some Thoughts Concerning Education.* Useful for a first use of an original document.

Emma Jacobina Christiana Marwedel (1818-1893)

A commitment to vocational education for women and the problems of working women led Marwedel to become interested in educational innovations, especially the kindergarten.

Marwedel served as the first director of the Girls's Industrial School in Hamburg, Germany; developed a plan for free cooperative school workshops; and studied with Friedrich Froebel's widow. After emigrating to America, she established a short-lived horticultural school on Long Island in 1870, followed by a successful kindergarten and training school in Washington, D.C., supported by James A. Garfield, John Sherman, and James G. Blaine. She moved to California with the help of Caroline Severance (founder of women's clubs) and established the Model Kindergarten and Pacific Model Training School for Kindergartners in 1876, the first in California and whose first graduate was Kate Douglas Wiggin. In 1880 she established the Pacific Kindergarten Normal School in San Francisco as well as several short-lived training schools in Oakland and Berkeley. Marwedel helped found the San Francisco Kindergarten Society, which established the first free kindergarten on the West Coast; was a founding member of the California Kindergarten Union; and opened an evening school for the vocational training of boys. A lecturer, author, and advocate for educational reform. She studied the work of Édouard Seguine, William Preyer, Francis Galton, and Henry Maudsley to develop a better understanding of the physical and psychological development of children.

Marwedel trained teachers who became leaders and reformers in the kindergarten movement. Her work helped establish kindergartens across the United States.

PRIMARY SOURCES

297. *Warum Bedurfen Wir Weibliche Gewerbeschulen und Wie Sollen Sie Angelegt Sein? Erlautert Vom Socialen Standpunkte Userer Zeit Von Emma Marwedel Oberleherin An Der Weiblechen Gewerbeschule In Hamburg.* [Why Do We Need Female Industrial Schools and How Should They Be Organized? Explained from the Social Point of View of Our Times by Emma Marwedel, Directress of the Women's Industrial School in Hamburg] Hamburg: H. Gruenig, 1868. Survey of women's working conditions and industrial schools in France, England, and Belgium. Presents a plan for developing free cooperative school workshops in Germany. One of two major publications by Marwedel.

298. *Conscious Motherhood; or the Earliest Unfolding of the Child in the Cradle,*
      Nursery, and Kindergarten. Boston: D.C. Health, 1889. Part I is by
      Marwedel and part II contains material by William Preyer from his psycho-
      physiological investigations of his own child called *"The Soul of the Child."*
      [Diue Seele des Kendes. Leipzig: Griebon, 1882] Sets forth a plan for
      child development and early education with Preyer's material, which might
      be called an early use of Piaget's method of studying one's own children.
      Stated that mothers must be trained in the kindergarten theory in order to
      help children develop to their fullest potential.

SECONDARY SOURCES

299. Barnes, Earl. "Emma Marwedel." In *Pioneers of the Kindergarten in*
      America. Prepared by the Committee of Nineteen. eds. Caroline D. Aborn,
      Catherine Watkins, and Lucy Wheelock. New York: Century & Co., 1924,
      pp. 265-269. Personal memories and a discussion of Marwedel's contri-
      bution to the establishment of the kindergarten in America. Written to
      encourage the spread of the kindergarten.
300. Swift, Fletcher H. *Emma Marwede, 1818-1893: Pioneer of the Kindergar-*
      ten in California. Vol. 6, number 3. Berkeley: University of California
      Publications in Education, 1931, pp. 139-216. Biography with footnotes
      and bibliography of material gathered from those who knew Marwedel.
      Discusses her work in establishing kindergartens in California.
301. Wiggin, Kate Douglas. *My Garden of Memory: An Autobiography.* Boston:
      Houghton-Mifflin, 1923, pp. 88-99, 100-114. Personal memories of
      Marwedel by one of her first American pupils. Presents a picture of meth-
      ods used with children and teacher training methods.

Margaret McMillan (1860-1931) and Rachel McMillan (1859-1917)

Convinced that the first six years of life were vital for the prevention of physical and emotional problems, the McMillan sisters founded the nursery school movement in England.

The McMillan sisters helped establish medical and dental care in neighborhood clinics in poor areas, with open-air camp schools to help children learn to live in a healthy way; The Rachel McMillan Training College in London; and parent education programs. They proposed the idea of nurture in education to deal with the child's complete development. The use of sensory and perceptual-motor training, the recognition of the importance of the child's imagination through self-expression experiences, teaching self-care skills, and the care of gardens and pets to teach responsibility, were educational programs they supported. They developed the concept of the nurse-teacher and organized the day around a flexible schedule, emphasing freedom of choice for children in activities and making the outdoors and freedom of expression an integral part of all daily activities.

The McMillan sisters influenced the theory and practice not only of nursery school education, but of the day care movement, which is its direct descendant. Their work on behalf of the poor helped to provide all young children with a head start in life.

PRIMARY SOURCES

302. *Early Childhood.* London: Swan Sonnenschein, 1900. Presents theories of child development and methods used during their years working in Bradford in the North of England. Describes the children's physical and cognitive development using the work of Edouard Seguine and Friedrich Froebel to outline a system of education for intellectual development through play, art, and movement.

303. *Education Through the Imagination.* London: Dent 1904, 1923 (rev.) Describes how working-class life (now called urban poverty) deprives children of creativity and suggests free movement and play as a way to help children develop ideas. Uses psychological and medical information to describe the use of psychology in education.

304. *The Camp School.* London: Allen & Unwin, 1917. Describes life in the open-air camp schools in poverty areas opened by the McMillan sisters and efforts to help children. Provides the beginning of a theoretical structure from the practical experience of establishing and running the early camp school.

305. *The Nursery School.* London: Dent, 1919. Describes the psychological and physical nurture necessary to help prevent disease through careful attention to food, clothing, personal habits, and early diagnosis of problems in the early childhood years.
306. *The Life of Rachel McMillan.* London: Dent, 1927. A biography of her sister which reveals much about Margaret. Describes the early clinic and camp school.

SECONDARY SOURCES

307. Bradburn, Elizabeth. *Margaret McMillan: Portrait of a Pioneer.* London: Routledge, 1989. Biography discussing McMillan's nursery school work in the context of current urban problems. Well documented.
308. Creswell, D'Arcy. *Margaret McMillan: A Memoir.* London: Hutchinson & Co., 1949. A memoir by the New Zealand poet with many pictures, but no bibliography or footnotes.
309. Lowndes, G.N.A. *Margaret McMillan: "The Children's Champion."* London: Museum Press Limited, 1960. A tribute to the celebration of the centenary of McMillan's birth. No bibliography, several pictures, an interesting list of contributors who provided information and memories.
310. Steedman, Carolyn. *Childhood, Culture, and Class in Britain: Margaret McMillan 1860-1931.* New Brunswick: Rutgers University Press, 1990. Excellent bibliography with discussions of McMillan's major works in context of her political beliefs. Provides a picture of early twentieth century Britain. Useful index and chapter notes. Not merely a collection of facts. Ends with, "Biographical Questions. Fictions of the Self," looking at biography and history.

Lucy Sprague Mitchell (1878-1967)

As cofounder of the Bureau of Educational Experiments, which later became the Bank Street School and in 1950 the Bank Street College of Education, Mitchell encouraged research on progressive education and educational experimentation.

Mitchell's efforts helped to provide an opportunity for professional women to pursue an interest in early childhood education in a scientifically rigorous way. She believed that theory and practice in education must never be separated, and that a commitment to the study of child development was necessary as the basis for early childhood curriculum. She developed teacher training techniques that combined educational theory, classroom practice, and research to stimulate creativity, and believed in educating the "whole" teacher to teach the "whole" child. She believed that children's block play and experiences in the neighborhood are the basis for map skills. Mitchell said that children develop play maps to orient their block communities and therefore map skills are a natural part of a child's thinking because they are used as a tool and a means of expression. Mitchell authored twenty books for children, including *Here and Now Stories* to stimulate language development and play with real experiences; was the author and editor of six books for adults and numerous articles for teachers; was renowned lecturer; and was director of the Writer's Workshop designed to encourage authors of childrens books.

Mitchell was a creative force who combined "the abilities of a scientist with the spirit of an artist."

PRIMARY SOURCES

311. "Imagination in Realism." *Childhood Education* 7, no. 3 (November 1931): 129-131. Discusses the importance of reality and imagination in children's literature. States that imagination is not fantasy nor the denial of reality, literature should present the real world on the maturity level of the reader to heighten the experience, reality must be familiar with the element of the "new," and children need contact with reality to "fly" from the here and now after many real experiences. Emphasizes that imagination enhances the real world of the child.

312. "Maps as Art Expression." In *Creative Expression: The Development of Children in Art, Music, Literature, and Dramatics,* ed. for the Progressive Education Association by Gertrude Hartman and Ann Shumaker. New York: John Day, 1932, pp. 40-41. Describes the beginning of map making as a floor activity scheme in block building and the progress children made to map orientation. States that play maps as expression and maps as tools are the same in children's minds and should not become divorced in

instruction. States that scientists can be artists and artists can be scientists if children have early, positive, natural map experiences.

313. "Children's Experiments in Language." In *Creative Expression: The Development of Children in Art, Music, Literature, and Dramatics,* ed. for the Progressive Education Association by Gertrude Hartman and Ann Shumaker. New York: John Day, 1932, pp. 167-177. Describes language development as evolving through distinct stages and possessing five characteristics. Provides examples of language development at each stage. States that educators must use the stages and characteristics to develop a "language pedagogy," but must not attempt to hasten the process of acquiring adult language patterns; children should be allowed to develop at their own pace.

314. *Young Geographers: How They Explore the World and How They Map the World.* New York: John Day, 1934; Basic Books, 1963; (repr.) Bank Street College of Education, 1991. (repr.) Describes how children learn geography from experiences with their environment. Provides a chart, "The Development of Geographic Thinking and Tools," showing how each age understands and uses geographic information. Includes curriculum implications for instruction. The photographs from the original 1934 edition are contrasted with updated photographs.

315. "Programming for Growth at P.S. 186." *Childhood Education* 22 (September 1945): 173-178 and 205. Describes how teachers at New York's P.S. 186 Manhattan developed the curriculum and instructional activities for their school with the help of the Bank Street workshops for teachers. The teachers developed a more integrated curriculum to better meet the needs of the students. Describes changes in several content areas and how the needs of individual students were met.

316. *Our Children and Our Schools: A Picture and Analysis of How Today's Public School Teachers are Meeting the Challenge of New Knowledge and New Cultural Needs.* New York: Simon & Schuster, 1951. Documentation of a cooperative effort between the Bank Street School staff and the New York City Board of Education starting in 1943 to provide in-service education. This is a study of the Bank Street workshops for teachers describing what schools are leaving behind and moving toward; public schools in action; strategies of workshop growth; curriculum building; learning through play experiences; growth of teacher's professional maturity; special work related to school problems; and what the future will bring. Provides a picture of how teachers effected change from within with the help of the workshop staff. Numerous pictures provided.

317. and Claudia Lewis, Virginia Schonborg, and Dorothy Stall. *Your Children in School.* New York: Macmillan, 1954. Presents "word sketches" taken from the Bank Street in-service teacher workshops and New York City schools to provide a glimpse of the problems and situations faced by teachers and children in real classrooms. Describes situations in kindergarten through grade 6 to help parents and teachers understand children's characteristics

and needs at various ages. Presents situations worth reading and discussing at the pre-service and in-service levels.

SECONDARY SOURCES

318. Antler, Joyce. *Lucy Sprague Mitchell: the Making of a Modern Woman.* New Haven: Yale University Press, 1987. A biography that highlights Mitchell's achievements as an educator, experimenter, writer, school founder, wife, and mother. Provides a list of Mitchell's writings for children and adults, archival sources, and extensive bibliographic notes. Two sections of photographs provide additional information.

319. "Lucy Sprague Mitchell is Dead; Founder of Bank Street College." *New York Times,* October 17, 1967, pp. 44, col. 2. Discusses Mitchell's contributions to education as a disciple of John Dewey, the founding of the Bureau of Educational Experiments, Mitchell's philosophy of education, her publications for children and adults, and her private life as the wife of Wesley Clair Mitchell.

Maria Montessori (1870-1952)

Montessori built on the work of Jean-Marc Gaspard Itard and Edouard Seguine to develop a child-centered approach to education. She created a program for young children in the slums of Rome which became known as the Montessori Method.

The innovations Montessori brought to early childhood education include the belief that each child develops from within as an individual; and that a child must be free to select and use materials with a minimum of adult interference for as long as desired. She invented self-correcting materials that developed the senses, language, the intellect, and the muscles; encouraged the use of child-size, moveable furniture; and the use of sensory materials to build the foundation for reading, writing, and arithmetic. Montessori advocated a change in the role of the teacher from a shaper of behavior to an observer of child development and the development of independence, self-care, and self-confidence through self-directed activities in an unhurried environment that was suited to the needs of the child.

Elements of the Montessori Method and adaptations of Montessori materials are used widely today in early childhood programs throughout the world. Montessori provided insight into and respect for the ways in which young children learn.

PRIMARY SOURCES

320. *The Montessori Method.* Trans. Anne E. George. New York: Frederick A. Stokes, 1912; New York: Schoken Books, 1964. (repr.) A detailed presentation of Montessori's theory and practice of education. The introduction to the 1964 edition by J. McVicker Hunt discusses the reasons for a reexamination of the Montessori Method.

321. *Pedagogical Anthropology.* Trans. Frederic Taber Cooper. New York: Frederick A. Stokes, 1913. Describes the systematic study of children for educational purposes and for developing philosophical principles of education. Discusses modern tendencies of anthropology and their relation to pedagogy; the principles of general biology; the anatomy of the child in detail; the biographical history of the pupil and his antecedents; and the application of biometry to anthropology for the purpose of determining the medial man. This is based on a series of lectures given at the University of Rome.

322. *The Advanced Montessori Method: The Montessori Elementary Material.* Trans. Arthur Livingston. New York: Frederick A. Stokes, 1917; Massachusetts: Bentley, 1964. (repr.) Describes the extension of the method for the education of children from age 7 through 11. Discusses methods for teaching grammar, reading, arithmetic, geometry, drawing, music, and

metrics. The appendices provide guidelines for child study and summaries of Montessori's lectures on pedagogy given in 1900 in Rome.

323. *The Secret of Childhood.* Trans. Barbara Barclay Carter. New York: Frederick A. Stokes, 1939. Discusses child development from the perspective of gaining an understanding of the child as a person to become "en rapport" with children. Describes: the physical, spiritual, intellectual, educational, and social development of the child. Concludes with a chapter called "Child as Master" describing the mission of parents and the rights of the child.

SECONDARY SOURCES

324. Davenport, Loretta Powell. *Maria Montessori, A. S. Neill, and Marva Collins: Educating for the Human Potential.* Ph.D. diss. Iowa State University, 1987. A discussion of Montessori's philosophical and educational ideas based on her upbringing. Her family encouraged her self-actualization and to share her life with others. States that Montessori saw teaching as an act of positive self-expression and demonstrated that even very young children could be taught to take control of their own learning. Bibliography of primary and secondary sources.

325. Kilpatrick, William Heard. *The Montessori System Critically Examined.* Boston: Houghton-Mifflin, 1914; New York: Arno Press, 1971. (repr.) A critical appraisal of the Montessori system written after Kilpatrick visited Italy to observe the system firsthand. Kilpatrick's description of the limitations of the system had a major negative impact on reactions to the importation of the system to America.

326. Kramer, Rita. *Maria Montessori.* New York: Putnam, 1976. A biography of Montessori with a critical analysis of her method and materials.

327. Sheehan, Joan Elizabeth (Sister Marie Chaminade Sheehan, O.P.) *A Comparison of the Theories of Maria Montessori and Jean Piaget in Relation to the Basis of Curriculum, Methodology, and the Role of the Teacher.* Ph.D. diss. St. John's University, 1969. Discusses Montessori's theory, methods, and the role of the teacher in her system of education. Extensive bibliography of primary and secondary sources.

328. Standing, E. M. *Maria Montessori: Her Life and Work.* London: Hollis and Carter, 1957; New York: New Amsterdam Library, 1962. (repr.) A classic biography with a critical examination of Montessori's contributions to education.

Robert Owen (1771-1858)

On his monument in a London cemetery the words "He Originated And Founded Infant Schools" commemorate Owen's work.

Owen's other contributions include raising the working age in his mill from six years to ten years and providing improved housing, better working conditions, and a company store that charged less than other shops for workers. In 1816 he established a school for children and adults in the mill in New Lanark, Scotland, called the Institute for the Formation of Character, which included an Infant School for children ages 3 through 6. Owen believed in the importance of the early childhood years. The school provided humane treatment for pupils by avoiding physical punishment; instruction aimed at the formation of good habits and kindness to others; play, outdoor activities, hands-on instruction, and field trips; and classes in reading, writing, arithmetic, writing, sewing, music, dance, geography, natural history, and modern and ancient history. Children were taught only what they could understand and were not forced to attend to lessons.

Owen's desire for social reform through model communities emphasized the education of children to deal with the new social order. The concept of Infant Schools spread to America and even though the movement was short-lived, it set the stage for future educational reforms. Infant Schools provided humane education and child care for working mothers.

PRIMARY SOURCES

329. Owen, Robert Dale. *Outline of the System of Education at New Lanark.* Glasgow: Wardlaw and Cunningham, 1824. Owen's son describes the education plan in detail for children in the mill town of New Lanark. Robert became his father's chief interpreter of educational ideas.
330. "Essay on the Formation of Character." In *The Life of Robert Owen by Himself.* Vol. 1. London: Effingham Wilson, 1857. Owen's educational philosophy and plan in his own words.
331. *The Life of Robert Owen by Himself.* 2 vols. London: Effingham Wilson, 1857-1858. Autobiography presenting Owen's political, social, and educational philosophies. Has reprints of Owen's writings until 1820 in the appendix.
332. Owen, Robert Dale. *Threading My Way: Twenty-Seven Years Autobiography.* New York: G.W. Carleton, 1874. The life of Owen's son with excellent original documents about New Harmony, the New Hampshire community based on New Lanark.

333. *New View of Society and Other Writings.* ed., G.D.H. Cole. London: J.M. Dent & Sons, 1927. Selection of Owen's works with a discussion of his plan for a better world, the theory of character formation, and the experiment in New Lanark. Uses New Lanark as the basis for Owen's community and educational plan.

SECONDARY SOURCES

334. Bestor, Arthur Eugene, Jr. *Backwoods Utopias: The Sectarian and Owenite Phases of Communitarian Socialism in America, 1663-1827.* Philadelphia: University of Pennsylvania Press, 1950. Discussion of Owenite community and other similar communities. Provides a background for understanding Owen's ideas on community life.
335. Cremin, Lawrence A. *American Education: The National Experience, 1783-1876.* New York: Harper & Row, 1980, pp. 74-100. Discussion of the New Harmony, New Hampshire community and Owen's philosophy, as well as other similar types of communities. Provides an excellent comparison of the New Lanark and New Harmony schools. Scholarly text with a useful bibliographic essay.
336. Harrison, John F.C., ed. *Utopianism and Education: Robert Owen and the Owenites.* New York: Teachers College Press, 1968. Selections of Owen's writings with several by his son Robert and one by his daughter, Jane. Introduction provides background and puts the original selections in perspective. Footnotes provide direction for further research.
337. Leopold, Richard William. *Robert Dale Owen.* Cambridge: Harvard University Press, 1940. Well-written biography of Owen's son.
338. Pitzer, Donald E., ed. *Robert Owen's American Legacy.* Indianapolis: Indiana Historical Society, 1972. The proceedings of the Bicentennial Conference for Owen's 200th birthday in 1971. Provides an excellent historical discussion of New Harmony and Owen's philosophy.
339. Silver, Harold. *Robert Owen on Education.* Cambridge: Cambridge University Press, 1969. Selections of Owen's educational writing. A very useful source.
340. Thompson, Keith Heathcote. *The Educational Work of Robert Dale Owen.* Ph.D. diss. University of California, Berkeley, 1948. Bibliography and discussion of the work done by Owen's son.

Elizabeth Palmer Peabody (1804-1894)

For Peabody to think was to act, and her actions laid the foundation for American early childhood education.

Peabody's wrote numerous articles and books about the philosophy, curriculum, and value of the kindergarten. She was editor and founder of *The Kindergarten Messenger;* gave international lectures; and, as a guest of the United States Commissioner of Education in 1871, served as referee on the subject of the kindergarten in discussions; which resulted in her writing the 1870 Commissioner of Education's annual report. Peabody encouraged students of Friedrich Froebel to come to America to organize schools and train teachers. She pestered Superintendent William Torrey Harris to establish public school kindergartens in Saint Louis; influenced the establishment of the kindergarten training department at what became Hunter College of the City of New York; encouraged widespread development of English language kindergartens and teacher training programs for White and Black teachers and children; and encouraged innovators.

Peabody's effort on behalf of the kindergarten was her greatest contribution to American education. While others were the true shapers of curriculum and practice, without "eccentric little Miss Peabody's irritating persistence," the kindergarten would not have had the exposure needed to gain public support.

PRIMARY SOURCES

341. and Mary Mann. *Guide to the Kindergarten and Intermediate Class and Moral Culture of Infancy.* Revised Edition. New York: E. Steiger, 1877 (rev.) The revised edition of the original book contains new insight based on visits to kindergartens in Europe. The new ideas helped Peabody realize that a book cannot make someone an expert kindergartner, only observation, experimentation, and firsthand experience can help someone develop the methods needed to teach young children. This guide is intended for experienced teachers. Contains object lessons, a description of the kindergarten, how to organize the room, and a section by Mary Mann that consists of seven letters of advice to a kindergarten teacher on the use of methods and materials. Also contains a section of kindergarten songs.

342. *Lectures in the Training Schools for Kindergartners.* Boston: D.C. Heath, 1886. A series of eight lectures presented to those training to teach kindergarten children. Includes discussions of the use of language, how to observe children, and the education of those who wish to become kindergartners. The appendix contains notes to the lectures, "The Song of the Weather," and "The Lord's Prayer." Provides view of early training methods.

343. "Letters From Miss Peabody to the Editor." In *Kindergarten and Child Culture Papers, on Froebel's Kindergarten with Suggestions on Principles and Methods of Child Culture in Different Countries,* ed. Henry Barnard. Hartford: Office of Barnard's *American Journal of Education,* 1890, pp. 5-16. A letter to Barnard praising his journal for providing American parents and teachers with an extensive discussion of the kindergarten which would help establish it permanently in America. Answers Bernard's request for help in selecting papers for his journal, describes the history of Froebel's work, Froebel's followers in Europe, and the establishment of the kindergarten in America.

SECONDARY SOURCES

344. Baylor, Ruth M. *The Contribution of Elizabeth Palmer Peabody to Kindergarten Education in the United States.* Ed. D. diss., New York University, 1960. A biography with excellent bibliography of primary and secondary sources for researchers. Published as *Elizabeth Palmer Peabody: Kindergarten Pioneer* (Philadelphia: University of Pennsylvania Press, 1965), with the bibliography easier to use.

345. Conrad, Susan. *Perish the Thought: Intellectual Women in Romantic America, 1830-1860.* New York: Oxford University Press, 1976. Describes Peabody as a women of letters who was better able than her outspoken sisters to make her ideas persuasive to society. Discusses Peabody as a romantic intellectual providing an alternative view of her contributions.

346. Ronda, Bruce A., ed. *Letters of Elizabeth Palmer Peabody: American Renaissance Woman.* Connecticut: Wesleyan University Press, 1984. Provides essays on each period in Peabody's life as introductions to the letters of that period. The letters to notable people provide insight into Peabody's personality and the causes to which she was committed. There are editorial comments, footnotes, location of the letters, and a general biographical introduction including pictures.

347. Ross, Elizabeth Dale. *The Kindergarten Crusade: The Establishment of Preschool Education in the United States.* Athens: Ohio University Press, 1976. Describes Peabody and the other women involved in the kindergarten movement as remarkable, well educated, and liberated. Provides a broader social context in which to examine the importance of the kindergarten to nineteenth century educational reform.

348. Shapiro, Michael Steven. *Children's Garden: The Kindergarten Movement from Froebel to Dewey.* University Park: Pennsylvania State University Press, 1983. A history of early childhood education, with bibliographic notes of value to the researcher.

349. Snyder, Agnes. *Dauntless Women in Childhood Education, 1856-1931.* Washington, D.C.: Association for Childhood Education International, 1972, pp. 31-56. Provides a biography of Peabody using many primary

and secondary sources. No bibliography, but complete footnotes. A standard source for the entire Kindergarten Movement written by someone who was involved in it.

350. Tharp, Louise Hall. *The Peabody Sisters of Salem.* Boston: Little Brown, 1950. A biography, written like a work of fiction, providing insight into the lives of Peabody and her sisters, Mrs. Horace Mann and Mrs. Nathaniel Hawthorne. Useful for researchers as a supplement. Bibliographic notes contain incomplete citations making them difficult to locate.

351. Vandewalker, Nina C. *The Kindergarten in American Education.* New York: Macmillan, 1908. A source that draws on the ideas and opinions of the author, who was a noted teacher trainer in the kindergarten movement. Although the bibliography is not complete, the book remains a valuable classic source for a researcher.

352. Weber, Evelyn. *The Kindergarten: Its Encounter with Educational Thought in America.* New York: Teachers College Press, 1969, pp. 18-19, 22, 24-27, 65, 220. An excellent source providing background and a bibliography of all the primary sources necessary for research.

Johann Heinrich Pestalozzi (1746-1827)

A belief that the best school for young children was similar to a firm, loving family led Pestalozzi to develop a new method of instruction that emphasized educational experiences based on emotional stability and warmth to foster self-development and positive moral growth.

Pestalozzi believed in individual differences and in extending educational opportunity to girls and the poor based on a belief that education should not be denied to anyone. His conviction that children should engage in activities that make them happy and his commitment to firsthand, positive experiences led to an emphasis on proceeding from the concrete to the abstract and from the general to the particular to fit instruction to the way children develop. He used real objects and object lessons to help children discover language, concepts, and numbers based on children's activities.

Sympathy and compassion were the foundation of Pestalozzi's method. Many visitors, including Friedrich Froebel, came to his school to observe his innovative way of teaching young children

PRIMARY SOURCES

353. *Die a Bendstude Eines Einsiedlers,* bearbeitet und mit Erlauterungen versehen von Karl Richter Leipzig: Padagogische Bibliothek, 1818. [*The Evening Hour of A Hermit*]. An attempt to analyze and justify his educational ideas after his failed experimental school called Neuhof, which was a working farm where students did household and farm work. Considering himself a failure as an educator, Pestalozzi writes about his experience in a flash of insight. This is a lesser known work than his *Leonard and Gertrude*, but is well worth reading.

354. *How Gertrude Teaches Her Children.* Trans. Lucy Halland and Francis Turner and ed. by Ebenezer Cooke. London: Allen & Unwin, 1894 (repr.) Syracuse: C.W. Bardeen, 1915. This work of fiction describes Pestalozzi's systematic method in which observation results in greater awareness, which results in speech and academic skills. It explores the ways in which a mother can help her children learn to count and read using daily activities such as household tasks, weaving, and spinning. Sequel to *Leonard and Gertrude.*

355. *Sammtliche Werke* Gesichtet (edited) von L.W. Seyffarth. 12 vol. Liegnitz: Habel, 1899-1902. [The complete works of Pestalozzi edited by L. W. Seyffarth] The complete writings in German.

356. *Leonard and Gertrude.* Trans. Eva Channing. Boston: D.C. Heath, 1906. This work written as a novel discusses how Gertrude saves herself and her seven children from her drunken, gambling husband by teaching her children to live in an orderly way. She becomes the center of the village and the lord who wants to reform the problem-ridden village seeks her help. Gertrude teaches by the way she acts and lives, not from theories.

357. *Letter of Early Education Addressed to J. P. Greaves, Esq.* Syracuse: C.W. Bardeen, 1906. Describes his method of teaching young children. The letters provide an interesting view of the method.

SECONDARY SOURCES

358. Baron de Guimps, Roger. *Pestalozzi: His Life and Work.* Trans. J. Russel. New York: Appleton, 1901. Presents Pestalozzi as a man of ideas in the context of his time. Good insight into Pestalozzi as a human being.

359. Monroe, Will S. *History of the Pestalozzian Movement in the United States.* Syracuse: C.W. Bardeen, 1907. Describes the spread of Pestalozzi's work in Europe and America and its interpretation by various noted educators, such as William Maclure, William Torrey Harris, and Henry Barnard. Provides an interesting bibliography.

360. Ulich, Robert. *History of Educational Thought.* New York: American Book Co., 1968, pp. 258-270. Provides a clear analysis of *The Evening Hour of a Hermit,* Pestalozzi's practical work, educational work, and social philosophy. An extensive bibliography is included.

361. Ulich, Robert. *Three Thousand Years of Educational Wisdom: Selections from Great Documents.* Cambridge: Harvard University Press, 1954, 1982 (rev.), pp. 480-507. Brief introductory discussion of Pestalozzi's life and work. Excerpts from *The Evening Hour of a Hermit* and *Leonard and Gertrude* provide a good introduction to Pestalozzi's writing.

Jean Piaget (1896-1980)

Using theoretical knowledge of biology and zoology and his postdoctoral work with Alfred Binet, Piaget developed an influential theory of how children think.

Piaget's theory of intellectual development provided early childhood educators with the following: the recognition of infancy as a critical period in cognitive development; the concept that the child is an active participant in the learning process from birth; the concept that cognitive development is divided into four distinct stages through which children go in a specific sequence at their own rate which is influenced by experience and maturation; and a change in the role of the teacher from an imparter of information to a designer of activities appropriate to a child's level of development, which allows them to act on materials and develop thinking skills. His theory provided a means by which to assess children's levels of intellectual functioning, intellectual readiness, and the appropriateness of classroom activities. Piaget's theory also helped parents to become more effective by looking at children's activities to assess what verbal and manipulative behaviors mean for the child. Educators can also access the numerous publications by a growing body of experts interpreting Piaget's theory and its implications for early childhood programs.

Piaget's work provided insight into how children's understanding of the world changes as they grow and what schools can do for young children. Piaget provided a new way of viewing the importance of the early years in the life of the child as the foundation for later learning.

PRIMARY SOURCES

362. *The Language and Thought of the Child.* Trans. Margorie Gabain. London: Routledge and Kegan Paul, 1926, 1932. (repr.). [*Le Langéage et la Pensée Chez L'Enfant* 1923.] A series of studies conducted in the 1921-22 school year in Geneva on logic in children describes the development and function of language and thought from age 2 to 11. Attempts to answer: "How does the child think? How does he/she speak? What are the characteristics of the child's judgement and reasoning?"

363. *Play, Dreams, and Imitation in Childhood.* Trans. C. Gattegno and F. M. Hodgson. New York: W.W. Norton, 1951, 1962. (rep.) Neuchatel Paris: Delachaux et Niestle, 1945 [*La Formation du Symbole Chez L'Enfant.*] Presents three case histories of children from birth through the early childhood stage describing the development of imitation, play, and unconscious symbolism.

364. *The Origins of Intelligence in Children.* Trans. Margaret Cook. New York: International Universities Press, 1952. [*Les Origines de la Pensée Chez L'Enfant,* Neuchatel Paris: Delachaux et Niestle, 1936.] Describes the growth of intelligence in six sequential stages: (1) the use of reflexes; (2) first acquired adaptations and (3) primary circular reaction; (4) secondary circular reaction and the child's procedures for prolonged spectules of interest; (5) the coordination of secondary schemata and the application to new situations; (6) tertiary circular reaction and the discovery of new ways through active experimentation and new ways by mental combinations.

365. "Jean Piaget." In *A History of Psychology in Autobiography,* eds. Edwin G. Boring, Herbert S. Langfeld, Heinz Werner, and Robert M. Yerkes. Vol. 4. Worcester, Mass. Clark University Press, 1952, pp. 237-256. An autobiography covering Piaget's life and work from 1896 to 1950. Insight into Piaget as a person and his own analysis of his work provides depth for the reader.

366. and Barbel Inhelder. *The Psychology of the Child.* Trans. Helen Weaver. New York: Basic Books, 1969. [*La Psychologie de L'Enfant.* Paris: Presses Universitaires de France, 1966.] A comprehensive summary of Piaget's work intended as an introduction to the longer studies. Discusses mental growth and behavior development up to the transitional phase of adolescence. Discusses all areas explored in previous studies in less technical terms provides a bibliography.

367. *Six Psychological Studies.* Trans. Anita Tenzer. New York: Random House, 1967. [*Six Études des Psychologie.* Geneve: Gonthier S.A., 1964.] A collection of six essays focusing on the development of behavior and thought, and the creation of logic, perception, and emotion. An introduction by David Elkind proves a good background.

368. *The Mechanisms of Perception.* Trans. G. N. Seagrim. New York: Basic Books, 1969. [*Les Mécanismes Perceptifs.* Presses Universitaires de Gravee, 1961.] An in-depth exploration of the development of perception. Presents twenty-five years of Piaget's field studies. Focuses on two problems: the relationship between perception and intelligence and the theory of perception compared to other forms of knowledge.

369. *Science of Education and the Psychology of the Child.* Trans. Derek Coltman. Paris: Denoel, 1969; New York: Orion Press, 1970. (repr.) Part I discusses education and teaching from 1935 through the 1960s describing advances in psychology and teaching methods. Part II, "New Methods: Their Psychological Foundations," traces the beginning of genetic psychology and its importance in education through the work of Jean-Jacques Rousseau, Johann Pestalozzi, Friedrich Froebel, John Dewey, Maria Montessori, Edouard Claparede, Ovid Decroly, William James, Alfred Binet, G. Stanley Hall, Arnold Gesell, Susan Isaacs, and other contributors to the understanding of how children learn.

370. and Barbel Inhelder in Collaboration with Hermine Sinclair-DeZwart. *Memory and Intelligence.* Trans. Arnold J. Pomerans. New York: Basic Books, 1973. [*Mémoire et Intelligence.* Paris: Presses Universitaires de France, 1968.] Discusses the connection between memory and intelligence in children, examining the way children remember additive and multiplicative logic structures. The studies examine whether memory operates on its own regardless of intelligence or if improvement in memory is based on progress in intelligence.

371. *Success and Understanding.* Trans. Arnold J. Pomerans. Cambridge, Massachusetts: Harvard University Press, 1978. [*Réussir et Comprendre.* Paris: Presses Universitaires de France, 1974.] Studies how action is controlled by thought when conceptualization catches up to action at about age 11, when thought begins to direct action and "to program it in advance." The goal of the studies is to "define the similarities of, and the differences between 'success' as the legitimization of 'know-how'; and 'understanding' as a characteristic of conceptualization regardless of whether it succeeds action or proceeds and guides it."

SECONDARY SOURCES

372. Almy, Millie. "Piaget in Action." *Young Children,* 31, no. 2 (January 1976): 93-96. States that Piaget is concerned with knowledge, not learning, and only a few of his articles deal with education. Piaget suggests that to apply his theories one must understand how the child makes a transition from infancy—the sensory-motor period to the concrete-operational thinking of childhood and to mature thinking in the stage of formal operations. Piaget claims that four factors help these transitions: maturation, action on the physical environment, social interaction, and the process of equilibration or self-realization. Almy describes how each factor can be applied to early childhood programs giving examples of activities. Concludes that "to put Piagetian concepts into action requires a thinking teacher (who)...looks beyond the child's verbalizations and manipulations and tries to understand what they mean to the child....This way of looking and thinking about children is not easy."

373. Bingham-Newman, Ann M. and Ruth A. Saunders. "Take a New Look at Your Classroom with Piaget as a Guide." *Young Children* 32, no. 4 (May 1977): 62-72. States that because Piaget's theory is an attempt to understand the child's logical reasoning and not an educational theory, it is applied in many ways in various programs of instruction. The authors claim that it is very difficult to apply Piaget's theory, however, it provides a framework from which teachers can be creative in its application. Lists principles of development derived from Piaget; the role of the teacher; and the concepts to be worked on. States that the Piagetian curriculum does not require expensive materials or drastic changes in the classroom.

Although activities can be separated for ease, development proceeds simultaneously in all parts. Concludes that children learn to do new things, be creative, and think creatively if teachers learn to apply Piaget's theory in the classroom.

374. Evans, Richard I. *Jean Piaget. The Man and His Ideas.* Trans. Eleanor Duckworth. New York: Dutton, 1973. A dialogue between Piaget and Evans in which many ideas and theories are discussed and clarified. Piaget tells how he developed his ideas, his early meeting with Sigmund Freud, and his views on the work of Noam Chomsky, Frederic Skinner, and Jerome Bruner. The introduction by David Elkind provides a summary of Piaget's theories, Piaget discusses genetic epistemology, and Evans makes observations on the dialogue style and gives an overview of the book. The book ends with an update of Piaget's autobiography (originally published in 1952).

375. Flavell, John H. *The Developmental Psychology of Jean Piaget.* New York: D. Van Nostrand, 1963. Provides a clear discussion of Piaget's theory and experiments, as well as a critique of his work. Intended for psychologists and those in related professions. Flavell provides biographical information in the introduction, a foreword by Piaget, and an extensive bibliography.

376. Gurth, Hans G. *Piaget for Teachers.* New Jersey: Prentice-Hall, 1970. Provides practical applications of Piaget's theory to classroom use. Describes Piaget's theory on language, thought, and motivation with classroom applications such as symbolic picture logic, thinking games, social thinking, musical thinking, creative thinking, and 180 school days of thinking written in letter form to teachers. Provides a glossary and a bibliography for further reading.

377. Gesell, Arnold L. "Review of J. Piaget, *Language and Thought in the Child.*" *Saturday Review of Literature* 5 (August 25, 1928): 72. States that "Piaget's book is an important scientific contribution because it undermines the inveterate intellectualism which the adult so naturally ascribes to the less sophisticated logic, but it is different from the adults. The difference is with the understanding." The review does not evaluate the book, it reports about it.

378. Gesell, Arnold L. "Review of J. Piaget, *Judgement and Reasoning in the Child.*" *Saturday Review of Literature* 5 (October 13, 1928): 208. States that "Professor Piaget has provided us with a valuable sequel to ... *Language and Thought in the Child.* Together these two volumes constitute what is in a sense the first systematic outline of the logic of children." Summarizes of the data and concludes that "although the text requires close reading, it is far from dull" and will be valuable to students.

379. Gesell, Arnold L. "Review of J. Piaget, *The Moral Judgement of the Child.*" *Saturday Review of Literature* 10 (October 7, 1933): 168. States that the book "explores the child's morality and demonstrates important parallels between moral and intellectual development," and that Piaget's work is

"distinctly European in flavor…Piaget's conclusions are not readily sum-
marized and his discussions sometimes seem over-detailed and recon-
dite."

380. "Jean Piaget Dies in Geneva at 84." *New York Times,* September 17, 1980, p.
1, col. 4 and p. D27. An obituary with excerpts from *Six Psychological
Studies.* Includes a photograph.

381. Kamii, Constance K. and Norma L. Radon. "A Framework for a Preschool
Curriculum Based on Some Piagetian Concepts." *Journal of Creative Behavior* 1, no. 3 (January 1967):314-324. States that compensatory preschool programs need to build a foundation for future intellectual development by using Piaget's sensory-motor period as its base to ensure that
no stage of development is skipped or only partially accomplished. The
"portions of Piaget's theory which appear to be essential for future academic achievement" are described in a preschool curriculum designed for
disadvantaged children. Two areas of cognitive development which the
authors consider "essential for logical thinking" are described in detail:
the representation of objects and the understanding of the relationship
among objects. The importance of building a program on these concepts
is described.

382. Schwebel, Milton and Jane Raph, eds. *Piaget in the Classroom.* New York:
Basic Books, 1973. A translation of Piaget's theory into classroom prac-
tice to help teachers more effectively integrate Piagetian concepts into
daily activities. Eleven authors provide chapters in sections dealing with:
The Development of the Mind; The Developing Child; and The Develop-
ing Teacher. Chapters include: "Language and Thought;" "Courage and
Cognitive Growth in Children and Scientists;" "The Use of Clinical and
Cognitive Information in the Classroom;" and "The Having of Wonderful
Ideas."

383. Sheehan, Joan Elizabeth (Sister Marie Chaminade, o.p.). *A Comparison of
the Theories of Maria Montessori and Jean Piaget in Relation to the
Basic Curriculum, Methodology, and the Role of the Teacher.* Ph. D. diss.
St. John's University, 1969. Discusses the foundations on which the cur-
riculum of early childhood education are based using the work of
Montessori and Piaget to illustrate key points.

384. Weber, Evelyn. *Ideas Influencing Early Childhood Education. Theoretical
Analysis.* New York: Teachers College Press, 1984, pp. 151-169. Describes
the recognition of Piaget's work; genetic epistemology; the stages of childhood development; preoperative thought; mechanisms of transition; and
Piaget's influence on early childhood education. Provides a comprehensive overview of Piaget, his theory, and its implications for practice.

Caroline Pratt (1867-1954)

The opening of the Play School in 1913 in Greenwich Village made Pratt's dream of a school in which young children were free to be creative and learn through play a reality.

Pratt believed that the teacher was an artist and teaching was a creative act and that the child was a seeking, expressive individual. This led to her conviction that a child's play was the foundation for learning while firsthand experiences were the basis for the curriculum. She held a life-long commitment to social reform and a strong belief in educational experimentation. She developed the Pratt blocks which were large wooden blocks that could be fastened together with wooden pegs to ensure that whatever was built would not fall apart. These blocks were used with wooden dolls with moveable joints and wagons for floor play and construction. Pratt advocated postponement of formal learning until age seven with the understanding that the child was an artist who recreated reality in his/her own way. She encouraged educators to use a job-related curriculum in which each age group had real work that taught subject matter based on a need to know. In 1916 Lucy Sprague Mitchell became a teacher at the Play School and Pratt became a member of the executive board of the Bureau of Educational Experiments of which Mitchell was the director. The Play School became the laboratory school of the Bureau of Educational Experiment and research in nutrition, language, record keeping and health care was conducted. In 1919 the Play School was renamed the City and Country School and Lucy Sprague Mitchell wrote the *Here and Now* stories for the children. The collaboration ended in 1930 when Pratt resigned from the Bureau of Educational Experiments and Mitchell moved her program to 69 Bank Street, also in Greenwich Village. Pratt shared her ideas through several books including *I Learn from Children.*

Pratt's unique ideas remain relevant and continue to influence early childhood education.

PRIMARY SOURCES

385. and Jessie Stanton. *Before Books.* New York: Adelphi Company, 1926. Describes teaching practices that develop skills before book learning begins. The use of direct experience as the basis for learning across the curriculum is presented. Advocates play as the basis for early learning.

386. and Lula E. Wright. *Experimental Practice in the City and Country School.* New York: Dutton, 1942. Describes the teaching methods and use of materials at the City and Country School in New York City. The purpose of

the school was to allow the individual child to expand, discover, and learn about the world through play and direct experiences with the world.

387. *I Learn from Children.* New York: Simon and Schuster, 1948; 1970 (Rep). Pratt's autobiography discusses how children learn, her philosophy, how she learned what children need by working with and observing them, the history of the City and Country School, and the education of parents.

SECONDARY SOURCES

388. Beck, Robert H. "Progressive Education and American Progressivism: Caroline Pratt." *Teachers College Record* 60 (December 1958): 129-137. Discusses Pratt's contributions to the Progressive Movement through biographical material and an analysis of her work.

389. Carlton, Mary Patricia. *Caroline Pratt: A Biography.* Ph. D. diss. Teachers College, Columbia University, 1986. Discusses Pratt's life and work using letters and material from colleagues. Bibliography of primary and secondary sources.

390. "Caroline Pratt, Educator, Dead: Founder of City and Country School was Early Exponent of Progressive Teaching." *New York Times,* June 7, 1954, p. 23. Pratt's obituary with emphasis on her contribution to early childhood education as a school founder.

391. Cremin, Lawrence A. *The Transformation of the Schools: Progressivism in American Education, 1876-1957.* New York: Knopf, 1961, pp. 201-207. Describes Pratt's life and work as the embodiment of the transformation of education by Progressivism into a new, scientific, child-centered education. Provides a biographical essay of primary and secondary sources.

392. Dewey, John and Evelyn Dewey. *Schools of Tomorrow.* New York: Dutton, 1915; 1943 (repr.); 1962, (repr.), pp. 86-91. Describes the materials, methods, curriculum, and school organization of the City and Country School as an example of an outstanding educational innovation.

393. Hirsch, Maxine Emelia. *Caroline Pratt and the City and Country School, 1915-1945.* Ph. D. diss. Rutgers University, 1978. Describes the City and Country School with emphasis on Pratt's philosophy. Bibliography of primary and secondary sources included.

394. Reich, Charles A. "Tribute to Caroline Pratt." *New York Times,* June 12, 1954, p. 14. Describes Pratt's life and work and her leadership at the City and Country School.

Alice Harvey Whiting Putnam (1841-1919)

Her desire to find the right way to educate her children led Putnam to organize a parents group to discuss Friedrich Froebel's *Mother Play and Songs* in 1874. This desire to learn more about Froebel's method through reading, discussion, and training changed Putnam's life.

Putnam took an active role in the development of early childhood education. After training with Anna Ogden, she opened a kindergarten in her home. She supervised the Training School of the Chicago Froebel Association from 1880 to 1910 at Cook County Normal School, transferring headquarters to Hull House to provide students with experience working with slum children. Art and science experiences were included in her training classes. Putnam was a teacher and director of the demonstration kindergarten at Cook County Normal School; a founding member of the Chicago Kindergarten Club and president in 1890; and a member and, in 1901, president of the International Kindergarten Union. She taught two courses as a nonresidential reader in education at the University of Chicago, as well as being an author and lecturer.

Putnam believed in kindergarten reform based on what was best for the children rather than strict adherence to Froebel's materials. A strong supporter of creativity and firsthand experiences, Putnam was against formal instruction in the kindergarten.

PRIMARY SOURCES

395. "Froebel's Message to Parents." *National Education Association Journal of Proceedings and Addresses 1889.* Topeka. Kansas Publishing House, 1889, pp. 473-478. Discusses Froebel's law of symbolism and analyzes it in relation to America in 1889, fifty years after he wrote *Die Mutter Und Kose Lieder.* This is an attempt to evaluate the significance of Froebel's advice to parents on early education.

396. "Shall Reading and Writing be Taught in the Kindergarten?" *Proceedings of the International Congress of Education of the World's Columbian Exposition, Chicago, July 25-28, 1893 Under the Charge of the National Education Association of the United States.* New York: National Education Association, 1895, pp. 327-328. States that there are definite stages of growth at particular periods of life in which we may do certain things, when we must work out certain problems which cannot be solved at any other time in life. The games, Gifts, and Occupations of the kindergarten are suited to the child's developmental stage and help the child gain information from the senses needed for further growth. Introducing reading at

the kindergarten stage deprives the child of the power of discovery by providing ready made ideas. The child must first discover the world before he/she is able to read about it. Makes a good case for late-twentieth-century parents and teachers to follow the needs of the children and not push for premature academic work.

397. "Conference on Training." *Proceedings of the Seventh Annual International Kindergarten Union Convention,* April 18-20, 1900, Brooklyn, New York. Chicago: Donnelley & Sons, 1900, pp. 96-137. The main topics of free Play and Simplicity in the kindergarten are discussed in papers by Patty Smith Hill, Mary Boomer Page, and Susan Blow's letter on free play. Under free play, comments concern its function and the function of kindergarten games, as well as the advantages and disadvantages of substituting traditional games for Froebel's. They ask: Does it admit of adult interference? Is the kindergarten the place for it? The discussion of Simplicity includes its role in work, in stories, and in games and songs. Also describes suggestions for further consideration at the next meeting.

398. "Work and Play in the Kindergarten." *National Education Association Journal of Proceedings and Addresses of the 40th Annual Meeting Held at Detroit, Michigan, July 8-12, 1901,* Topeka, Kansas: Kansas Publishing House, 1901, pp. 502-507. Discusses the connection between work and play in kindergarten activities. States that kindergarten children move naturally between these two types of activities and this is indicative of their developmental stage. Educators must recognize this developmental characteristic and plan for it in the kindergarten curriculum. Lists four of Froebel's principles which describe the necessity for a balance between work and play in response to the child's stage of development.

399. "How Froebel Planned to Foster the Child's Powers in Language." *National Education Association Journal of Proceedings and addresses of the 41st Annual Meeting Held at Minneapolis, Minnesota, July 7-11, 1902;* Topeka, Kansas: Kansas Publishing House, 1902, pp. 417-425. Describes Froebel's ideas on language acquisition in the context of the psychological information of the day, including John Dewey's theory. Discusses the significance and value of the Mother Play and nursery rhymes in language acquisition. Presents what can be considered a very late-twentieth century discussion of the role of the parent-child dialogue and play as the basis for language and concept development. There is discussion of Putnam's presentation "How Froebel Planned to Foster the Child's Powers in Language" by Elizabeth Harrison, J. N. Crouse, Sarah C. Brooks, and several other discussants. Putnam responds by describing the experience at Hull House, where babies were left without an adult to guide their play and language development. After a kindergarten teacher was employed to work with the children aged 15 months to 2 years for an hour each morning and afternoon, there was a difference in language use noted.

400. "Drawing in the Kindergarten." *National Education Association Journal of Proceeding and Addresses of the 46th Annual Meeting Held at Cleve-*

land, Ohio, June 19-July 3, 1908, Winona, Min.: National Education Association, pp. 523-526 Putnam concluded that Froebel's drawing suggestions are not good for kindergarten age children although these suggestions can be used at a later stage of development. Putnam states that Dewey believed that every mode of expression no matter how impressionistic or mechanical has two sides, the idea and the technique. Putnam states that long before children have knowledge of technique they express an idea no matter how vague or crude. Putnam provides examples of how young children express a concern for symmetry and suggests that kindergarten children can use stencils, transparent slates, and arranged sticks to make pictures. Proposes that art in the kindergarten should express ideas and sincere feelings. Children's work Putnam states may be crude at this stage, but it should not be ugly. The medium, or the conditions, or the teacher should help the child create something genuine.

401. "The Coordination of the Kindergarten and the Elementary School." *National Education Association Journal of Proceedings and Addresses of the 46th Annual Meeting Held at Cleveland, Ohio, June 29-July 3, 1908,* Winona, Min.: National Education Association, 1908, pp. 537-539. Putnam is the discussant of a paper by Dr. Gregory, a superintendent of schools who described a break between the kindergarten and the elementary school. Putnam describes her methods for developing a coordination between the two levels, providing specific suggestions and examples from Froebel's work. She states that the child is a growing organism who is happy and develops through creative activity at every level. Describes schedules, equipment, and activities to encourage the creativity at both levels.

SECONDARY SOURCES

402. "Alice H. Putnam." *Kindergarten and 1st Grade Magazine* (March 1919): 111-115. Presents information on Putnam's life and work as a memorial tribute.

403. "Evolution of the Kindergarten Idea in Chicago. Mrs. Alice H. Putnam and the Froebel Association." *Kindergarten Magazine* 5, no. 10 (June 1893): pp. 729-733. Describes the twenty year history of the first kindergarten study class in Chicago and the growth of the kindergarten movement. Describes the establishment of the Chicago Free Kindergarten Association and the Chicago Froebel Association, names pioneers, and lists Putnam's contributions to the founding of the Chicago movement.

404. Newell, Bertha Payne. "Alice H. Putnam." In *Pioneers of the Kindergarten in America Prepared by the Committee of Nineteen, The International Kindergarten Union.* New York: The Century Co., 1924, pp. 204-222. A memoir of Putnam as a kindergarten pioneer providing personal insight into Putnam as a defender of children rather than a strict interpreter of Froebel's philosophy.

405. "Putnam, Alice Harvey Whiting." *Biographical Dictionary of American Educators.* Ed. John F. Ohles. Vol. 2. Westport, CT: Greenwood Press, 1978, p. 1065. Biographical sketch of Putnam's life and work in the Chicago Kindergarten Club, The Froebel Association, at the Correspondence Department of the University of Chicago, and at Cook County Normal School.

406. "Putnam, Alice Harvey Whiting." *Notable American Women. A Biographical Dictionary* ed. Edward T. James. Vol. 3. Cambridge, Massachusetts: Belknap Press of Harvard University Press, 1971, pp. 105-106. Provides biographical information and a discussion of Putnam's work in the Chicago Kindergarten movement. Describes her contributions at Hull House, Cook County Normal School, the University of Chicago, the International Kindergarten Union, and the Froebel Association.

407. Ross, Elizabeth Dale. *The Kindergarten Crusade: The Establishment of Preschool Education in the United States.* Ohio: Ohio University Press, 1976, pp. 46, 54-55, 63, 69-70, 95. Describes Putnam's connection with Francis W. Parker and the Cook County Normal School, her training classes held at Hull House, and her brief training of Kate Douglas Wiggin. States that Putnam was an innovator "who did not follow Froebel's precise system, but worked out variations."

408. Shapiro, Michael Steven. *Children's Garden,: The Kindergarten Movement from Froebel to Dewey.* University Park: The Pennsylvania State University Press, 1983, pp. 113, 115-117, 121, 155-156. Describes Putnam's commitment to child study and states that she was considered a radical leader whom Susan Blow excluded from an 1894 meeting because of her views. Goes beyond biographical information. Provides endnotes with primary and secondary sources.

409. Vanderwalker, Nina C. *The Kindergarten in American Education.* New York: Macmillan, 1908; New York: Arno Press and The New York Times, 1971, (repr.) pp. 18, 60, 66, 112, 154. Discusses Putnam's contributions to the kindergarten movement stating that "the whole kindergarten movement in Chicago grew out of a class formed by Mrs. Alice H. Putnam in 1874 for the study of Froebel." Describes the growth of the Chicago Kindergarten Association and the kindergarten movement, stating that "the names of Mrs. Alice H. Putnam, Kate Douglas Wiggin, Patty S. Hill…and many others are known to every kindergartner in the land."

410. Weber, Evelyn. *The Kindergarten: Its Encounter with Educational Thought in America.* New York: Teachers College Press, 1969, pp. 47-48, 69, 95, 124. Describes Putnam as one who always maintained independence in curriculum development and interpretation, providing her students with direct contact with slum children by moving her training classes into Hull House and warning against extreme reliance on Froebel's formal materials. States that Putnam attempted to incorporate activities in science and art into the curriculum and believed in progressive reform of the kindergarten based on child study and Dewey's philosophy.

Jean-Jacques Rousseau (1712-1778)

The publication of *Émile* in 1762 called attention to the importance of the early childhood years and changed the history of education.

Rousseau's contributions to education include the suggestion that young children need motor activity, firsthand experiences, and happy games to develop language, mathematical and sensory concepts. He believed in the natural goodness of children and opposed the artificial lifestyle of the times, especially the way children were raised as small adults. He suggested that young children be protected from society and allowed to engage in activities that were natural for children; children should be allowed to become fully developed or mature before exposing them to society; they should have the freedom to play and be spontaneous; and he advocated a study of how children develop at different ages as the basis for educational practice. Rousseau proposed that formal learning activities be delayed until age 12 and suggested that educators use motivating activities to ensure attention and interest. He believed that young children should gain self-acceptance and discipline from the natural consequences of things and activities.

Rousseau's naturalism emphasized freedom, growth, interest, and activity as the basis for early education. His ideas were radically different from the eighteenth century concept of education which may be the reason that the application of Rousseau's ideas to classroom practice had to wait for others more involved with practice rather than theory.

PRIMARY SOURCES

411. *Émile, Ou de L'Éducation en Oeuvres Completes*, eds. Bernard Gagnebin and Marcel Raymond. Vol. 4. Bibliothéque de la Pléiade, Gallemard: Paris, 1959-1969. [*Emilius: or a Traité of Education, Translated from the French of J.J. Rousseau, Citizen of Geneva*. Edinburgh, Dickson & Elliot 1773. *Émile: or Education*. Trans. Barbara Foxley. New York: E.P. Dutton & Co., 1911. *Émile for Today*. Trans. William Boyd. London: Heinemann, 1956. *The Émile of Jean-Jacques Rousseau*. Trans. and ed. William Boyd. New York: Teachers College Press, 1962. *Émile or on Education*. Trans. Allan Bloom. New York: Basic Books, 1979.] Written as a novel, the book describes the life of a fictional child from birth to marriage. Provides a guide to raising a child in a natural way with the father as the tutor, guide, and mentor away from society, which Rousseau believed to be corrupting. As a result of *Émile*, childhood began to be treated as a separate time of life and children were no longer expected to conform to adult styles of dress and standards of behavior. The Boyd and Bloom translations provide excellent notes and introductions.

SECONDARY SOURCES

412. Cranston, Maurice. *Jean-Jacques: The Early Life and Work of Jean-Jacques Rousseau, 1712-1754.* Chicago: University of Chicago Press, 1982. *The Noble Savage: Jean-Jacques Rousseau, 1754-1762.* Chicago: University of Chicago Press, 1991. Discusses Rousseau in the context of his times, stating that we now have a clearer picture of him and his ideas as a result of better scholarship. These are the first two volumes of what will be a trilogy. Cranston tells readers that he went to primary sources to "break the chain of books based on books." Provides notes rather than a bibliography.

413. Ulich, Robert. *History of Educational Thought.* New York: American Book Co., 1968, pp. 211-224. Discusses Rousseau's social and educational ideas and provides an evaluation of his work. States that it is as difficult to evaluate the historical significance of Rousseau's written work as it is to evaluate his educational philosophy. Concludes that Rousseau deserves the attention of people who can preserve their own judgement and not regard his writing as gospel. Very useful bibliography.

414. Ulich, Robert. *Three Thousand Years of Educational Wisdom: Selections from Great Documents.* Cambridge: Harvard University Press, 1954, 1982 (rev.), pp. 383-425. A brief comment on Rousseau's educational philosophy with selections from *Émile* translated in 1773.

Alice Temple (1871-1946)

A leader in the progressive kindergarten reform movement, Temple interpreted John Dewey's philosophy for classroom practice.

Temple studied with Anna E. Bryan and worked as a teacher and principal at the Chicago Free Kindergarten Association (1885-1904). She taught, and became director, of the kindergarten department at the University of Chicago; and organized the first university kindergarten-primary department at the University of Chicago in 1913 establishing a three-year program, which became a four-year bachelor's degree program setting a pattern for universities throughout the country. She was active in the International Kindergarten Union and its successor Association for Childhood Education as committee member, chairperson, and president (1925-1927). Temple worked for inclusion of a kindergarten division in the United States Bureau of Education. She tested unified kindergarten-primary methods at the University of Chicago laboratory school for eleven years before recommending its adoption in *Unified Kindergarten First Grade Teaching*. She was also a successful author, lecturer, and teacher trainer.

Temple developed with Samuel Parker a program for early childhood education which was scientific, contemporary, and provided a method that used problemsolving, skill development, creativity, and habit formation.

PRIMARY SOURCES

415. "The Factor of Environment in the Making of a Kindergarten Program." *Kindergarten Review* 19, no. 17 (October 1908): 77-81. States that the environment of the kindergarten determines the experiences and the curriculum of the program. Presents three questions to help determine learning experiences and concludes by stating that the kindergarten must connect home and school to ensure that there is no break in the child's development. The kindergarten program must be based on the social and physical environment of the children enrolled in the program.

416. "Problems in the Administration and Supervision of Student Teaching." *Childhood Education* 1 (May 1925): 430-434. A report of responses to a questionnaire on teacher training sent to state Normal Schools and teachers colleges in 1924. Discusses data in terms of three problems: inadequacy of training school facilities; organization of practice teaching; and specific methods of directing practice teaching. Concludes by asking, "Would a handbook on the goals of practice teaching be of value?"

417. and Parker, Samuel Chester. *Unified Kindergarten and First Grade Teaching*. Boston: Ginn and Co., 1928. Presents an integrated discussion of

theory and classroom practice to describe the curriculum and activities at
the University of Chicago Laboratory School over a sixteen-year period.
This classic was intended for in-service and pre-service teachers. It describes materials, equipment, classroom organization, and activities in the
primary program based on Dewey's philosophy.

418. "Value of Supervision from the Standpoint of the Teacher." *Childhood Education* 4 (March 1928): 315-317. A report of data gathered in 1927 on
teachers' statements about what supervisors do that is helpful to teachers.
A list of statements and their frequency is presented and compared with a
study done with a larger group of teachers. Presents a surprisingly contemporary (1990s) discussion of the needs of teachers and how supervisors help them deal with problems.

419. "Extending the Child's Social Understanding." *Childhood Education* 5 (April
1929): 419-423. Describes the development of a planned, sequential social studies curriculum for the primary grades based on experiences appropriate for each age group to help children develop social behavior and
social understanding.

420. "The Kindergarten in America—Modern Period." *Childhood Education* 13
(April 1937): 358-363 and 387. Presented as a tribute to the 100th anniversary of the founding of the kindergarten, Temple reviews the changes
in the kindergarten program. She discusses the beginnings of reconstruction, Dewey's educational experiment, the development of the Progressive kindergarten, the influence of the Montessori Method, the relation of
the kindergarten to the school, the advent of the nursery school; and the
kindergarten and the Association of Childhood Education (which was the
International Kindergarten Union).

SECONDARY SOURCES

421. "Alice Temple Dead." *New York Times,* January 7, 1946, p. 19. A discussion
of Temple's life and contributions to the kindergarten movement.

422. "Alice Temple Dies." *Chicago Tribune,* January 7, 1946, p. 16. An obituary
tribute to Temple's life and work in Chicago.

423. Snyder, Agnes. *Dauntless Women in Childhood Education, 1856-1931.*
Washington, D.C.: Association for Childhood Education International,
1972, pp. 189-229. A biography and discussion of Temple's contributions to the development of a restructured kindergarten program based on
Dewey's philosophy.

424. Weber, Evelyn. *The Kindergarten: Its Encounter with Educational Thought
in America.* New York: Teachers College Press, 1969, pp. 124-126, 135-
137. Discusses Temple's contributions to developing a scientific basis for
primary school curriculum and methods.

425. Weber, Evelyn. *Ideas Influencing Early Childhood Education: A Theoretical Analysis.* New York: Teachers College Press, 1984, pp. 86-88, 100.

101. Discusses Temple's ideas as part of the kindergarten reconstruction movement and the strong influence of Dewey's ideas on Temple's philosophy.

Mary Church Terrell (1863-1954) and
The National Association of Colored Women

Terrell believed that educating young children would build the foundation for future generations.

After graduating from Oberlin College Terrell taught at Wilberforce University and in the District of Columbia's black public schools. She continued as a lecturer after her marriage. As the first president of the National Association of Colored Women, Terrell continued her work in education through the development of projects for children. Terrell used her leadership, knowledge of teaching, and her teaching to encourage the development of kindergartens and nursery schools for black children throughout the United States.

Through the National Association of Colored Women and its local clubs, African-American women made the following contributions to early childhood education: model kindergartens were established in Washington, D.C. in 1896; in 1896-1898 the Washington Colored Woman's League established a Normal School managed by Anna Evans Murray to train teachers for six free kindergartens; Mothers' Meetings were developed to provide information on childcare for working women; the donations of clothing and shoes; and the establishment of kindergartens throughout the South. Club work in New York, Chicago, and Detroit established kindergartens to assist with the immigration from rural South to urban centers. Anna Evans Murray appealed before Congress and received the first federal funds for kindergartens. Frances A. Joseph established the first kindergarten for black children in New Orleans. Other efforts by African-American women resulted in the establishment of day nurseries in Philadelphia and Englewood, New Jersey; orphanages and settlement house programs; the National Training School for Colored Girls in Washington, D.C., for employment skills; teacher training schools at centers such as Tuskegee, and a variety of community social services programs.

Gerda Lerner (1972) states that "the history of the black woman's contribution to education during and after Reconstruction remains to be written." The work of the club women under the leadership of Terrell is a vital part of that history. Specific club women's lives need further research, however, their commitment to early childhood education was truly pioneering work.

PRIMARY SOURCES

426. Atlanta University. *Annual Second Conference for the Study of Problems Concerning Negro City Life May 25-26, 1897.* ed. W.E.B. Du Bois. Atlanta: Atlanta University, 1897. Reports given by Lucy C. Laney on the

Motherhood Congress discuss marriage and the home with emphasis on child rearing; Rosa Morehead Bass discusses the need for kindergartens in Atlanta providing examples of the importance of early childhood education. Resolutions adopted by the conference include the need for kindergartens to be established and maintained.

427. Terrell, Mary Church. "The Duty of the National Association of Colored Women to the Race." *AME Church Review* (January 1900): 340-354. Describes the efforts of the National Association of Colored Women since its 1896 founding to execute its plans especially on behalf of children. Discusses the importance of kindergartens and day nurseries.

428. Murray, Anna J. "A New Key to the Situation." *The Southern Workman* 29 (September 1900) pp. 503-507. An address delivered at the Hampton Conference in July 1900. Proposes the kindergarten as the right kind of education at the right age to solve the problem of inequality among the races. Describes Murray's successful efforts to secure funds for the establishment of kindergartens for black children in Washington, D.C., through the Senate Appropriations Committee. Describes the success in teacher training efforts to provide teachers for southern kindergartens.

429. Terrell, Mary Church. "What Role is the Educated Negro Woman to Play in the Uplifting of Her Race?" In *Twentieth Century Negro Literature or Relating to the American Negro—By 100 of America's Greatest Negroes.* ed. D. W. Culp, Toronto: J. L. Nichols 1902, pp. 172-177. Discusses the role women must play to improve the lives of African-Americans. Discusses the efforts of women's clubs in helping children in early childhood through improved living and educational conditions.

430. Dunbar, Alice. "A Kindergarten Club." *Southern Workman* 32 (1903): pp. 386-390. Describes a kindergarten club for young children established as part of a charity mission on the upper east side of New York City. Tells about the problems and successes of a kindergarten without a trained teacher in crowded conditions lacking materials.

431. Murray, Anna E. "In Behalf of the Negro Woman." *Southern Workman* (April 33, 1904): 232-234. States that black and white women will solve racial inequality when black women are trained to be kindergarten teachers and the kindergarten becomes the basis for all education. The kindergarten will provide the foundation for higher education and a common cause for cooperation among the races for the benefit of children.

432. Yates, Josephine Silone. "Kindergarten and Mother's Clubs as Related to the Work of the National Association of Colored Women." *Colored American Magazine* 8 (1905): 304-311. Describes the efforts of the National Association of Colored Women to establish kindergartens and mothers' clubs throughout the United States for the benefit of black children. Discusses the training of teachers, the existing kindergartens, and the plan used by the Leavenworth, Kansas, Mother's Club.

433. Emerson, Helena Titus. "Children of the Circle. The Work of the New York Free Kindergarten Association for Colored Children." *Charities* (Octo-

ber 7, 1905): pp. 81-83. Describes the kindergarten and after school clubs of the association in New York City.

434. Griffin, Maude K. "The Hope Day Nursery." *Colored American Magazine* 10, (1906): 397-400. Describes the founding in 1902 of the Hope Day Nursery with the help of Mr. and Mrs. Arthur M. Dodge and presided over by a committee of black women of greater New York. Discusses the establishment, population, daily schedule, fund raising efforts, and assistance given by clients.

435. "Efforts for Social Betterment Among American Negroes; Report of a Social Study Made by Atlanta University Under the Patronage of the Trustees of the John F. Slater Fund; Together with the Proceedings of the 14th Annual Conference for the Study of Negro Problems, held on Tuesday May 24, 1909 Atlanta Georgia." ed. W.E.B. Du Bois. Atlanta: Atlanta University Press, 1909, no. 134, pp. 118-127. Describes the Gates City Kindergarten Association and efforts to establish kindergartens in other areas of the United States.

436. Reed, Pearlie. "Spelman College Nursery School." *Spelman Messenger* 46 (1930): 12-14. The nursery school was established to provide for the educational needs of preschool children, to train teachers, and to offer research opportunities for professionals concerned with the physical, intellectual, emotional, and social development of young children. Describes the physical facilities, daily schedule, and importance of the school.

437. Shivery, Louis. *History of Organized Social Work Among Atlanta Negroes, 1896-1935.* Master's thesis, Atlanta University, 1936. Provides a history of the Gates City Free Kindergarten Association in Atlanta using primary sources such as the annual reports of the association.

438. Terrell, Mary Church. *A Colored Woman in a White World.* Washington, D.C.; Ransdell, 1940. Autobiography with a preface by H. G. Wells. Provides insight into the problems faced by African-American women from the 1860s to the 1930s.

439. Chittenden, Elizabeth F. "As We Climb. Mary Church Terrell." *Negro History Bulletin,* February-March, 1975, 38, pp. 351-354. A biography discussing Terrell's achievements in club work, women's suffrage, and civil rights.

440. White, Gloria M. "Mary Church Terrell: Organizer of Black Women." *Integrated Education* (September-December 1979 and December 1980): 2-8. Biography of Terrell and a discussion of the founding and work of the National Association of Colored Women. Extensive bibliography.

SECONDARY SOURCES

441. Anderson, James D. *The Education of Blacks in the South 1860-1935.* Chapel Hill: University of North Carolina Press, 1988. Excellent bibliography. Provides a discussion of education for African-Americans within a politi-

cal, economic, and cultural context. Discusses teacher training in the early twentieth century. No discussion of the kindergarten movement.

442. Ashelman, Mary Miller. *The Virginia Pattern of Education for Children Under Six in Historical Perspective.* Ph. D. diss. Virginia Polytechnic Institute and State University, Virginia, 1984. Excellent section on the contribution of black educators to early childhood education starting with a pre-Civil War discussion of education for black Americans. Excellent bibliography which includes primary sources.

443. Beatty, Barbara. "Child Gardening: The Teaching of Young Children in American Schools." In *American Teachers: Histories of a Profession at Work,* ed. Donald Warren. A publication of the American Educational Research Association. New York: Macmillan, 1989, pp. 65-97. Discusses the kindergarten with reference to black educators' contributions to the kindergarten movement. Excellent endnotes.

444. Cahan, Emily D. *Past Caring: A History of United States Preschool Care and Education for the Poor, 1820-1965.* New York: National Center for Children in Poverty, School of Public Health, Columbia University, 1966. Describes early forms of preschool care and education in the 1920s and the 1930s; the professions and children; the federal role: a series of crisis interventions; and care and education in the 1960s. Extensive bibliography.

445. Collier-Thomas, Bettye. "The Impact of Black Women in Education: An Historical Overview." *Journal of Negro Education* 51, no. 3 (Summer 1982): 173-180. Presents a discussion of the contributions of black women to education, stating that research in this area is difficult because there are few book-length publications about the women or their work. Calls on researchers to focus on these women and their contributions. Concludes with a table listing nineteen women in education with a very brief description of each accomplishment. This issue of the journal is devoted to "The Impact of Black Women in Education." It is a good starting point for research in this area.

446. Cunningham, Charles E. and D. Keith Osborn. "A Historical Examination of Blacks in Early Childhood Education." *Young Children* (March 1979): 20-29. Extensive bibliography. Provides insight into the work done by unsung black pioneers in kindergarten and nursery school education.

447. Davis, Marlanna W., ed. *Contributions of Black Women to America. Volume II, Civil Rights, Politics and Government, Education, Medicine, Science.* Columbia, S. C.: Kenday Press, 1982. Provides a discussion of the contributions of black women to education at all levels, including pioneers in early childhood.

448. Hamilton, Tullia Kay Brown. *The National Association of Colored Women, 1896-1920.* Ph. D. diss. Emory University, Atlanta, 1978. Provides an overview of the National Association of Colored Women; profiles of club women; the work of the association; attitudes on sex and race, and a summary and conclusion. Excellent bibliography.

449. Jones, Beverly Washington. "Quest for Equality: The Life and Writings of Mary Eliza Church Terrell 1893-1954." In *Black Women in United States History,* vol. 13, ed. Darlene Clark Hine. New York: Carlson, 1990. Biography and selections from Terrell's writings. Excellent bibliography of primary sources.

450. Lerner, Gerda, ed. *Black Women in White America: A Documentary History.* New York: Vintage, 1972. Provides primary sources are introduced by Lerner's comments and an excellent bibliographic essay by Lerner.

451. Neverdon-Morton, Cynthia. *Afro-American Women in the South and the Advancement of the Race, 1895-1925.* Knoxville: University of Tennessee Press, 1989. Provides a discussion of the 1896 Atlanta Conference on the social and physical conditions of Negroes in cities, and the decision to emphasize the kindergarten as a basis for education in Atlanta. Provides a brief discussion of the Gates City Free Kindergarten Association. Extensive endnotes with primary sources.

452. Scott, Anne Firor. *Natural Allies: Women's Associations in American History.* Chicago: University of Illinois Press, 1991, pp. 141-158. Presents a discussion of how women, black and white, worked for political and social advancement through organizations such as the National Association of Jewish Women, the National Association of Colored Women's Clubs, and the Daughters of the American Revolution. Excellent bibliographic notes. Chapter 6 places emphasis on the educational efforts of the National Association of Colored Women's Clubs.

453. Tank, Robert M. *Young Children, Families and Society in America Since the 1920's: The Evolution of Health, Education, and Child Care Programs for Preschool Children.* Ph.D. diss. University of Michigan, 1980. Provides information on the history of child care with a discussion of the efforts of intervention for children in poverty. Extensive bibliography.

454. Wesley, Charles Harris. *The History of the National Association of Colored Women's Clubs: A Legacy of Service.* Washington, D.C.: Mercury Press, National Association of Colored Women's Clubs, 1984. A history of the association from its founding to activities in the 1980s. Provides profiles of officers past and present. There is a brief bibliography.

Edward Lee Thorndike (1874-1949)

Thorndike was a pioneer in experimental psychology and the measurement of educational outcomes. His ideas were very far removed from those of Friedrich Froebel and it was not until after extensive laboratory testing in the 1920s that they were accepted by the kindergarten movement.

The translation of Thorndike's work into practice in the restructuring of the kindergarten was done in a variety of ways. The development of precise goals; the development of an inventory of habits that stated how to measure changes in behavior; changes in activities to reflect desirable changes in conduct and skills development; a connection between kindergarten and the first grade to measure continuous growth; the use of individual and group problemsolving as the means for developing desired conduct through meaningful experiences; and the kindergarten report card which remains today as an inventory of desirable habits.

Thorndike's ideas changed the structure of the kindergarten and modern early childhood education by introducing educators to the importance of a scientific theory of learning.

PRIMARY SOURCES

455. "Notes on Psychology for Kindergartners" *Teachers College Record* 4 (November 1903): 45-76. Provides a discussion of the application of psychological principals to the education of young children. Discusses the relation of mind to body life; mental health; the relation of mental life to muscular contraction; mental growth; native tendencies; habit (including the general dynamics of mental life); inhibitions; the influence of special forms of training on general abilities; and modern means of measuring mental traits. Concludes with a description of the ways in which the kindergarten is changing methods in response to new scientific ideas. Presents a comparison of the 1889 kindergarten and the 1901 kindergarten to show the changes in methods, materials, and content.

456. *Principles of Teaching Based on Psychology.* New York: Seiler, 1906. Class lectures from Teachers College published as a complete book on scientific methods of teaching. Thorndike states that the aim of the book is to "make the study of teaching scientific and practical." Chapters cover The Teacher's Problem; Psychology and the Art of Teaching; Physical Education; Interests and Capacities; Appreciation; Interests; Individual Differences; Attention; Reading; Motor Expression; and concludes with Testing: The General Results of Teaching, General Results of School Work,

and a Scientific Study of School Work. A bibliography of classic sources is included.

457. *The Elements of Psychology.* New York: Mason-Henry Press, 1907; Seiler, 1913. (repr.) A text designed as an introduction to the general principles of psychology. Includes: The Subject Matter and Problems of Psychology; Descriptive Psychology; The Psychological Basis of Mental Life; Physiological Psychology; and Dynamic Psychology. Concludes with a discussion of the relations of psychology to other sciences, the arts, personal conduct, and the science of psychology as a whole.

458. *An Introduction to the Theory of Mental and Social Measurement.* New York: Teachers College, 1913. A classic reference book in mental measurement and statistical theory.

459. *Education: A First Book.* New York: Macmillan, 1923. An introduction to education intended to help students understand educational psychology and sociology; the history of the theory and practice of education; methods of teaching and classroom management; and the relationship of philosophy and ethics to education. The book is intended for beginning students of education and discusses the meaning and value of education; the aims of education; material for education—facts and laws, the nature of man, the learning process; the means of education; methods of education; and the results of education. Also cover specifically education in the United States, discussing students, teachers, organization, curriculum, and the fiscal aspects of education.

460. *Educational Psychology: Briefer Course.* New York: Teachers College, 1914. A single volume covering the original nature of man, the psychology of learning; and individual differences and their causes. This is a simpler version of the original three volume work intended for college and Normal School students.

461. and the Staff of the Division of Psychology of the Institute of Educational Research of Teachers College, Columbia University. *The Fundamentals of Learning.* New York: Teachers College, 1932; AMS Press, 1971. (repr.) The report of a three-year study of the facts and forces of learning done by Thorndike and colleagues, funded by a Carnegie Corporation Grant.

SECONDARY SOURCES

462. "Annotated Chronological Bibliography of Publications by E. L. Thorndike, 1898-1925." *Teachers College Record* 27 (February 1926): 466-515. Annotations were made by colleagues of Thorndike from universities such as Teachers College, Rutgers, New York University, and Johns Hopkins. Provides a comprehensive source of Thorndike's early and influential works on the occasion of his twenty-fifth anniversary at Teachers College.

463. Cattell, J. McKeen. "Thorndike as Colleague and Friend." *Teachers College Record* 27 (February 1926): 461-465. A personal tribute from a colleague

on Thorndike's twenty-fifth anniversary at Teachers College. Provides insights into Thorndike as a person as well as a pioneer psychologist.

464. Cremin, Lawrence. *The Transformation of the School: Progressivism in American Education, 1876-1957.* New York: Knopf, 1962, pp. 110-115, 172, 176, 185-186, 369-370. A discussion of Thorndike's influence on education and as part of the Progressive Movement. The biographical notes clearly connect Thorndike to Progressive education.

465. Goodenough, Florence L. "Edward Lee Thorndike 1874-1949." *The American Journal of Psychology* 62 (April 1950): 291-301. A memorial tribute to Thorndike which includes biographical information, a brief chronological discussion of his writings, and a concluding summary of the value of his contributions. This includes a picture with Thorndike's signature below it.

466. Hainer, Frank Thomas. *A Critical Analysis of the Thought of Edward L. Thorndike: The Logical Status of "Scientific" Claims in Education.* Ph.D. diss. University of Pittsburgh, 1977. Provides a bibliography of primary and secondary sources. Traces Thorndike's scientific influence on education.

467. Joncich, Geraldine M., ed. *Psychology and the Science of Education: Selected Writings of Edward L. Thorndike.* Classics in Education, no. 12. New York: Teachers College Press, 1962. Provides a comprehensive introduction with biographical material and an analysis of Thorndike's contributions. Selections from sixteen of Thorndike's books and articles are presented with brief introductions to provide perspective for the reader.

468. Lorge, Irving. "Edward L. Thorndike's Publications From 1940-1949." *Teachers College Record* 51 (October 1949): 43-45. An updated and enlarged bibliography published after Thorndike's death. This is not annotated, but it provides the student and researcher with a complete list of Thorndike's works when used with the other two bibliographies published by *Teachers College Record* (see no. 462 and no. 469).

469. "Publications From 1898-1940 by E. L. Thorndike." *Teachers College Record* 41 (May 1940): 699-725. This is a revised and updated bibliography developed for students to celebrate Thorndike's fortieth anniversary at Teachers College. This was compiled by the Division of Psychology at the Institute of Educational Research at Teachers College (see no. 462 and no. 468).

470. Roche, Lawrence Anthony. *A Comprehensive Study of the Idea of the Science of Education in the Works of John Dewey and Edward L. Thorndike.* Ph. D. diss. Case-Western Reserve University, 1969. Discusses the philosophies of both pioneers and their influence on education. Bibliography of primary and secondary sources provided.

471. Woodworth, Robert S. "Edward Lee Thorndike, 1874-1949." In *Biographical Memories,* Vol. 27. Washington, D.C.: National Academy of Sciences of the United States, 1952, pp. 209-237. A scientific and personal biography of Thorndike which includes Thorndike's vita, a picture, and a com-

plete bibliography of primary works including a 1950 publication of his
last article.

Evangeline H. Ward (1920-1985)

Ward served on the governing board of the National Association for the Education of Young Children (NAEYC) longer than anyone else as a board member and as president from 1970-1974.

Ward held many other distinguished positions. She was president of the U.S. National Committee of the World Organization for Early Childhood Education; executive director of Child Development Consortium; director of the Institute for Teachers of Disadvantaged Children at Temple University; chairperson of the Department of Early Childhood Education, Hampton Institute; executive director of the Nursery Foundation of St. Louis Comprehensive Day Care Service Agency; coordinator of the Department of Early Childhood Education, Temple University; director of Model Head Start Training for the U.S. Office of Economic Opportunity; director of the Office of Education; and NDEA Institute for Pennsylvania state school superintendent. In addition, she was a consultant for the National Council for Accreditation of Teacher Education (NCATE) and the Educational Testing Service; she worked on the revision of the national teachers examination on early childhood education, the Colloquy on Black Child Development, Model Cities—Philadelphia Program; and the Pennsylvania White House Conference on Children and Youth. Ward served as delegate to the 1976 White House Conference on Children and was a member of dozens of organizations, including the Pennsylvania Black Council on Higher Education, the British Association for the Education of Young Children, and the National Conference on Black Child Development. She was an international speaker and author.

Ward helped build the foundation from which NAEYC expanded to provide national services to parents, teachers, and better opportunities for all children.

PRIMARY SOURCES

472. "A Child's First Reading Teacher: His Parents." *Reading Teacher* 23 (May 1970): 756-760. Develops the idea that the first teachers in a child's life are his/her parents, who help develop the environmental experiences, skills, concepts, and feelings that he/she brings to school. This pre-reading stage is the base on which the educational system will build. Provides examples of how parents and the family help children learn from vital experiences and develop skills for reading success. Describes programs such as Head Start and Follow Through, which mandate parental involvement. Concludes that there must be a coordinated effort to recognize all influences on learning.

473. "From the President." *Young Children* 29 (April 1973): 184-194. Discusses
the guiding principles for the National Association for the Education of
Young Children, using her participation in the first conference of the National Council on Black Child Development held in Washington, D.C., in
January 1973. Reports that Dr. Charles Hamiliton of the Russell Sage
Foundation discussed the difference between the necessary strengths for
institution building and programmatic approaches. Reveals that those who
are elected to the national office view NAEYC from an institutional building strategy, while members tend to view it as a programmatic model.
"Institution building implies *Acting* rather than *Reacting!* The NAEYC
purpose: to act upon the rights and serve the needs of children." Describes
the hazards of institution building and states that a deliberate design is
necessary. It includes all aspects of the organization and requires all members to work together to build NAEYC.

474. "The Making of a Teacher: Many Disciplines." In *Teacher Education of the
Teacher, by the Teacher, for the Child. Proceedings from a Conference
Sponsored by the National Association for the Education of Young Children.* ed. Bernard Spodek. Washington, D.C.: NAEYC, 1974, pp. 45-54.
Discusses the process of becoming a teacher by describing: What is teaching? How many roles? and What knowledge do we use when learning to
be teaching individuals? The discussion concludes with William G. Carr's
statement that what teachers need to do is "test all the attributes needed to
teach." Extensive bibliography is included.

475. "The Child Development Associate Consortium's Assessment System." In
Early Childhood Education, It's an Art? It's a Science? ed. J. D. Andrews.
Washington, D.C.: National Association for the Education of Young Children, 1976, pp. 149-164. Highlights and summaries of the material presented in 1974 (see no. 474). *Young Children* 31, no. 4 (May, 1976): 244-
245. Describes the process of assessing the competencies of child care
personnel and granting credentials to those found to be competent to work
in day care and child development centers. Poses and answers numerous
questions, such as What is a child development associate, (CDA)? How
does an individual become a CDA? What are the basic features of the
consortium's assessment system? How is the consortium funded? Provides a competency structure chart of the CDA person.

476. "A Code of Ethics. The Hallmark of a Profession." In *Teaching Practices:
Reexamining Assumptions,* ed. Bernard Spodek. Washington, D.C.: National Association for the Education of Young Children, 1977, pp. 65-69.
Also in *Ethical Behavior in Childhood Education, Expanded Edition* by
Lillian H. Katz and Evangeline Ward. Washington, D.C.: National Association for the Education of Young Children, 1978; 1989,(repr.) pp. 17-26.
Discusses the need for a code of ethics for the early childhood education
and development profession and efforts to develop the code by identify-
ing "an appropriate ethical stance." Ward questions: How should you, as

an early childhood practitioner, respond to this situation? What is your ethical responsibility or stance when "just one more child" is added to a group? Presents an initial Code of Ethics for Early Childhood Educators. Concludes that interest in the code is only the beginning of deep and provocative issues. "Membership in NAEYC is the arena for the continued pursuit and ultimate adoption of a Code of Ethics."

SECONDARY SOURCES

477. "Dr. Evangeline Ward, 1920-1985." *International Journal of Early Childhood* 17, no. 2 (1985): 77-79. The journal of the World Organization for Early Childhood Education, Organisation Mondial pour l'Education Prescolair expresses shock and sorrow at the sudden death of Dr. Ward while participating in the Australian Early Childhood Association Triennial Conference in Brisbane. Details Ward's work for OMEP and her international efforts on behalf of young children. Several letters in French, English, German, and Spanish are included. A memorial fund was established by the U.S. National Committee in Ward's name.

478. "Evangeline H. Ward, 65, Education Specialist." *Philadelphia Inquirer,* October 25, 1985, p. D12. An obituary highlighting Ward's work at Temple University, her teaching experiences, and her presidency of NAEYC and the National Council for Black Child Development. States that Ward died in Australia during a conference. Gives details of the memorial service.

479. "Evangeline H. Ward, Was Active in Senate." *Temple Times,* October, 31, 1985. Obituary with a 1979 photograph detailing Ward's work at Temple University, national service in NAEYC and National Council for Black Child Development. Details of a Memorial Service are discussed.

480. "In Memoriam." *Young Children* 41 (November 1985): 57. A memorial tribute from NAEYC detailing Ward's work in the organization and her dedication to early childhood education. Discusses her post-doctoral study at Oxford University and the University of St. Andrews in Scotland.

481. Temple University News Release, December 2, 1970. Announces Ward's election to the presidency of the 18,000 member NAEYC. Presents a discussion of Ward's work at Temple, her educational background, and lists her address in Philadelphia.

Lillian Weber (1917-1994)

Knowledge of the realities of life in urban classrooms led Weber to work with New York City teachers. Her goal was to help teachers organize learning so that the classroom became more responsive to the ways in which young children learn.

Weber made many contributions to early childhood education. She helped to organize the Open Corridor Program at New York City College, as well as helped establish the City College Advisory Service to train selected teachers to assist others in reorganizing their classrooms, and the Workshop Center for Open Education at City College. She was a founding member of the North Dakota Study Group, a National Organization for research on change in schools, a member of the boards of the National Consortium on Testing and Prospect Archives and Center for Education and Research, and the first woman invited to deliver the annual John Dewey Lecture in Chicago. She led a government educational study mission to China in 1977. Weber also led seminars in Australia, Israel, Norway, Germany, Kenya, and Tanzania. She was the winner of the 1986 City College Gold Medal as City Woman of the Year.

The Workshop Center continues to provide urban teachers with support, training, and inspiration to educate young children. Weber's dream of matching the classroom to the needs of the students to provide the best educational experience possible is still alive.

PRIMARY SOURCES

482. *The English Infant School and Informal Education.* New Jersey: Prentice-Hall, 1971. Discusses the theory and practice observed in British primary schools during an eighteen-month study tour. Presents a history of the infant school and material on the work of Susan and Nathan Isaacs, Basil Bernstein, and Jerome Bruner. A classic.

483. "Some Lasting Impressions of English Practice." In *The Open Classroom Reader.* ed. Charles E. Silberman. New York: Random House, 1973, pp. 22-26. Describes the activities and the skills that children develop in an open classroom setting as well as the physical and educational environment of an English infant school.

484. "The Rational of Informal Education." In *The Open Classroom Reader,* ed. Charles E. Silberman. New York: Random House, 1973, pp. 148-166. Discusses the history of open education describing the influence of Jean Piaget, and Susan and Nathan Isaacs.

485. "Planning for the Free Day." In *The Open Classroom Reader,* ed. Charles E. Silberman. New York: Random House, 1973, pp. 352-361. Describes the

underlying structure to what appears to be an unstructured chaotic classroom. States that there is a plan in the open classroom based on materials and activities and the children's use of these.

486. "Dealing with Reality: The Open Corridor Approach." In *The Open Classroom Reader,* ed. Charles E. Silberman. New York: Random House, 1973, pp. 467-480. Describes how Lillian Weber started the open corridor project and how teachers are helped to develop the theory and practice of open education. States that the program was started to help teachers who wanted to try a new classroom organization and developed into a learning community of children and teachers working and learning together.

487. "The Classroom Community and the Need to Communicate." In *The Open Classroom Reader,* ed. Charles E. Silberman. New York: Random House, 1973, pp. 541-550. States that the best way to teach reading and writing skills in the open classroom is in a community of people who communicate with each other in a variety of activities. Children need an environment in which many activities can be used to learn and practice skills in groups with others who have similar interests.

488. "Adapting Classrooms for *All* the Children." In *Special Education and Development,* ed. Samuel J. Meisels. Baltimore: University Park Press, 1979, pp. 65-89. Discusses the ways in which the open classroom provides an appropriate setting for children with a variety of special needs. Provides information on inclusion, heterogeneous grouping, mainstreaming, and behavior problems and the ways in which the open classroom mirrors the heterogeneous nature of society.

489. "Books to Nourish Democratic Educators." In *Progressive Education for the 1990's: Transforming Practice,* eds. Kathe Jervis and Carol Montag. New York: Teachers College Press, 1991, pp. 185-187. Weber describes how she relates fiction and nonfiction to her ideas about education because all books contain ideas that support the "psychological and physical space needed for developing the human capacities of *all* the children, the parents, the teachers, and the strengths of the communities where they all live." Provides examples from works such as *My Mother's House, The Learning Tree, Go Tell It on the Mountain;* and *Foxfire Books.* Includes a bibliography.

490. "Reexaminations: What *IS* the Teacher and What *IS* Teaching?" In *To Become a Teacher Making a Difference in Children's Lives,* ed. William Ayers. New York: Teachers College Press, 1995, pp. 127-152. This is Weber's last written work. She discusses changes in schools and critiques the last twenty-five years under the headings: Giving Precedence to What the Teacher Is and What the Teacher Commitments Are; First Changes and Reassessments; Further Reexaminations: Continuing Obstacles to Change; and The Imperatives of Continuing Action and Reflections. Concludes that we must examine what is and what is not there in light of what is seen as the result of a small change. One must constantly reexamine

how children's learning is affected by "teacher's commitment, clarity of commitment, and the teaching process that results from it."

SECONDARY SOURCES

491. Hazelwood, Ann C. and Martha A. Norris. "The Open Corridor Program: An Introduction for Parents." In *Open Education: A Sourcebook for Parents and Teachers,* eds. Ewald B. Nyquist and Gene R. Hawes. New York: Bantam Books, 1972, pp. 237-250. A description of the program initiated by Weber at the City College of New York. Presents information for parents to help them understand open education and become involved in it. Describes how children would learn; what the teacher does; the role of parents and children in learning; a history of the program; and questions frequently asked by parents. Contains a list of recommended readings.

492. Hechinger, Fred M. "Maybe the Testers Can't Read." *New York Times,* March 26, 1972, sec. 4, p. 9. A report of Weber's analysis of standardized reading tests that concludes that reading success is assessed more accurately by teacher observation than by standardized test results. Taken from *Notes from City College Advisory Services on Open Corridors,* March, 1972, the newsletter of New York City College's Workshop Center on Open Education.

493. "In Memoriam: Lillian Weber." *Young Children* 50 (November 1994): 57. A memorial tribute to Weber discussing her life and contributions to the open education movement in America.

494. "Lillian Weber, 77, Educator and Expert in How Young Learn." *New York Times,* February 24, 1994, p. D.20. An obituary presenting brief information about Weber's life and work at the City University on open education.

495. Schnier, Walter and Miriam Schnier. "The Joy of Learning in the Open Corridor." *New York Times Magazine,* April 4, 1971, p. 30ff. A discussion of the founding and work of Weber's Open Corridor Program at City College with background on open education programs throughout the United States. Written for the general public.

Lucy Wheelock (1857-1946)

Founder of Wheelock College, Wheelock was a leading figure in the kindergarten movement.

Wheelock advocated a gradual evolution of Friedrich Froebel's principles and materials. She founded Wheelock Kindergarten Training School in 1896. She served as second president and founding member of the International Kindergarten Union; was a member and chairperson (1905-1909) of the Committee of Nineteen, and one of the editors of the final report *The Kindergarten* in 1913; worked with, and in 1908 served as chairperson of, the National Congress of Mothers, which became the National Congress of Parents and Teachers; and served on the joint committee of the International Kindergarten Union and the National Education Association (1913-1918); and was a member of the Education Committee of the League of Nations. Wheelock visited eight southern states in 1916 on a Mothers' Crusade to establish kindergartens. She was also a prolific author, coauthoring with Elizabeth Colson, *Talks to Mothers;* translating *Red Letter Stories* and *Swiss Stories for Children* by Johanna Spyre; and writing a weekly newspaper column called "Hints To Teachers." She organized the free kindergarten at Hope Chapel for Black children in Boston and worked with settlement houses and organized a kindergarten at South End House connected to the Wheelock Training School. Wheelock contributed to early childhood education as a lecturer, author, and community activist on behalf of establishing kindergartens for all children.

In 1941 the Wheelock Kindergarten Training School became Wheelock College.

PRIMARY SOURCES

496. "Symbolism in Teaching." *Sunday School Teacher* 31 (November 16, 1899): 46. Wheelock explains Froebel's use of symbolism and that "these truths must be made objective in objects the child constructs."

497. "The Kindergarten Gifts." *Kindergarten Review* 10 (December 1899): 107-108. Describes the use and importance of Froebel's Gifts in the kindergarten program.

498. "Report of the Committee of Nineteen." *Proceedings of the Fourteenth Annual Meeting of the International Kindergarten Union,* April, 1907, New York City. Cleveland, Ohio: Electric Printing Co., 1907, pp. 41-49. Identifies six topics which cause variation in practice. (1) Adherence to Froebel and Froebelian philosophy. (2) The theory of play, and the relation of play to work. (3) The place of instinct in early education. (4) The sense image versus the idea. (5) The doctrine of interest as applied to the kindergarten

program. (6) Symbolism and the Mother-Play. Each subject is discussed. Wheelock states that "this ... summary of topics, which have forced themselves upon our consideration from the present kindergarten situation, is offered not for the purpose of more sharply defining differences, but as an effort towards the discovery of the reconciling view, which shall enable us to strengthen our work and ... our influence as educators."

499. "The Changing and Permanent Elements in the Kindergarten." *Proceedings of the Seventeenth Annual Meeting of the International Kindergarten Union, April 27-29 1910,* St. Louis, Missouri. Woburn, Mass: Andrews Printers, pp. 206-218. Describes various changes that have influenced the kindergarten program such as G. Stanley Hall's child study movement, and John Dewey's work. States that there are four elements which have remained constant. An emphasis on the principal of self-activity. The interrelation or interaction or relationship of the human being, as a child of nature, a child of man, and a child of God, as well as the relationship between the child and his/her environment, physical, social, and spiritual. The idea of development as growth and the belief in stages of growth— that each stage has its own requirements which should be met by educational guidance. The ideas of education as guidance toward and understanding of self to nature and union with God. "Methods and devices may cease, materials may be done away" but these elements remain constant.

500. *Talks to Mothers.* Boston: Houghton-Mifflin, 1920. Advice to mothers about child development and behavior. Discusses the healthy child, the obedient child, and the good child. The last chapter, The Thoughtful Mother, tells that the best way to be a good mother is to observe and learn from one's children. Lists several ways to learn from children: the scientific way; the way teachers test progress; and the "watchful observation of one who wishes to know the meaning of all that she sees." Provides information from G. Stanley Hall, James Marc Baldwin, and in the appendix, on Methods of Studying Children, Wheelock suggests reading William James. Concludes by suggesting cooperation between mothers and teachers.

501. "Preface." In *Pioneers of the Kindergarten in America.* Authorized by the International Kindergarten Union. Prepared by the Committee of Nineteen. New York: The Century Co., 1924, pp. xi-xii. Describes the contents of each chapter, praises contributors for the personal touch and states the aim of the book is to promote the aims of the International Kindergarten Union: to provide information about the kindergarten movement; to advocate the rights of childhood; and to maintain high standards.

502. "Miss Peabody As I Knew Her." In *Pioneers of the Kindergarten in America.* Authorized by the International Kindergarten Union. Prepared by the Committee of Nineteen. New York: The Century Company, 1924, pp. 26-38. Wheelock provides a personal portrait of Elizabeth Palmer Peabody as an advocate of the kindergarten and describes her contributions.

503. "Tribute to Kate Douglas Wiggin." *Pioneers of the Kindergarten in America.* Authorized by the International Kindergarten Union. Prepared by the Com-

mittee of Nineteen. New York: The Century Co., 1924, pp. 296-298. Wheelock presents a memorial to the life and work of Wiggin as a true pioneer.

504. and Caroline D. Aborn. *The Kindergarten in New England.* Presented at the Swamp Scott Convention of the Association for Childhood Education, June 26-30, 1935. Washington, D.C.: Association for Childhood Education, 1935. Discusses the history of the kindergarten tracing it through New England. Describes key figures and their contributions to the kindergarten movement.

505. and Caroline D. Aborn, and Sharah A. Marbel. *The History of the Kindergarten Movement in the Mid-Western States and in New York.* Presented at the Cincinnati Convention of the Association for Childhood Education, April 19-23, 1938. Washington, D.C.: Association for Childhood Education, 1938. Presents a history of the kindergarten in Ohio, Illinois, Wisconsin, Michigan, Missouri, Minnesota, Iowa, Indiana, Kentucky, Tennessee, New York State, and New York City. Describes the contributions of pioneers in each state to the kindergarten movement.

SECONDARY SOURCES

506. "A New Building for Kindergarten Education." *Kindergarten Review* 25, no. 6 (February 1915): 379. Describes the 1914 move to a new building which became Wheelock School and later Wheelock College's permanent home.

507. Bain, Winifred E. *Leadership in Early Childhood Education: Images and Realities. A History of Wheelock College, 1888-1889 to 1963-1964.* Prepared for the 75th Anniversary of Its Founding as Wheelock School. Boston: Wheelock College, 1964. Provides a historical overview of Wheelock College from its founding to 1964 and a biography of Wheelock in the context of her work in the International Kindergarten Union and in teacher training.

508. Head, Linda R. "Lucy Wheelock." *Those Intriguing Indomitable Vermont Women.* Montpelier: Vermont State Division of the American Association of University Women, 1980, pp. 27-28. A biography, with photograph, highlighting Wheelock's academic and professional achievement.

509. Leeper, Mary E. and Jean Betzner. "Lucy Wheelock." *Childhood Education* 23 (January 1947): 247. An obituary with photograph discussing Wheelocks contributions to early childhood education.

510. Liddle, Elizabeth Ann, ed. *Wheelock College 100 years: 1888–1889 to 1988–1989.* Boston: Wheelock College, 1989. Chapters by Evelyn Weber, Marian Wright Edelman, Sharon Lynn Kagan, and Barbara Beatty, photographs, and biographical information provide a history of Wheelock's Kindergarten Training School which evolved into Wheelock College. The various authors discuss Elizabeth Peabody, Henry Barnard, and other leaders in the kindergarten movement putting Wheelock's work into perspec-

tive and highlighting her contributions. Footnotes and references provide
the history of early childhood education in America.

511. "Lucy Wheelock," *Who Was Who in America.* Chicago: Marquis, Vol. 2:
1950, p.570. A brief biography including the names of several of
Wheelock's publications.

Kate Douglas Wiggin (1856-1923)

In 1878 Wiggin started the Silver Street Kindergarten in San Francisco, the first free kindergarten west of the Rockies.

Wiggin was a prolific author, writing books for children, including *The Story of Patsy* and *Rebecca of Sunnybrook Farm,* as well as professional books for teachers, including a three-volume study of Froebelian principles and practices. She wrote articles to enlighten the public and raise money for the establishment of kindergartens and was an international lecturer. Wiggin advocated teacher training with emphasis on the language arts; was a pioneer in the spread of kindergartens in western states; worked for more freedom in the use of materials and methods to suit pupil needs; and worked to have kindergartens written into the San Francisco city charter and developed two experimental kindergartens there between 1880 and 1886. She was one of the founders of the Golden Gate Kindergarten Association and lobbied for free kindergartens for the poor. The graduates of her training program started most of the kindergartens in the western states.

Miss Kate, teacher of the "Kids Guards" (as the word kindergarten was mispronounced) on Silver Street, describes the lives of children and the importance of free kindergartens in meeting their educational and daily living needs.

PRIMARY SOURCES

512. *The Story of Patsy.* Privately published, 1883. Based on Wiggin's kindergarten teaching experience with poor children this story serves as propaganda for the benefits of kindergarten education. Published to raise money for the Golden Gate Kindergarten Association.

513. and Nora Archibald Smith. *Froebel's Occupations.* Boston: Houghton-Mifflin, 1896. Interpretation of Friedrich Froebel's work connecting his philosophy with many examples from the reality of teaching. Provides quotes from John Dewey, G. Stanley Hall, and Herbert Spencer, who offer criticism of Froebel's ideas. Provides both the Froebelian and alternative perspectives on kindergarten practice. Wiggin appears to favor a less rigid use of the materials.

514. and Nora Archibald Smith. *Children's Rights.* Boston: Houghton-Mifflin, 1896. Discusses the problems and the necessity of building a bridge between the adult world and that of the child. Practical illustrations are given.

515. and Nora Archibald Smith. *Kindergarten Principles and Practices.* Boston: Houghton-Mifflin, 1896. A discussion of Froebel's ideas with insights from Wiggin's teaching experience. Based on her teacher training lectures.

516. and Nora Archibald Smith. *Froebel's Gifts.* Boston: Houghton-Mifflin, 1899. Based on her lectures for teachers, Wiggin discusses the Gifts and concludes that with more subtle observation of children educators may need to make "radical changes in the objects which are Friedrich Froebel's legacy to the kindergarten." Provides insight into how Wiggin used the materials with the children she taught.

517. *Posy Ring.* Boston: Houghton-Mifflin, 1903. Poems for children organized for bedtime, quiet-time, playtime, seasons, and Christmas by William Blake, William Shakespeare, Alfred, Lord Tennyson, William Wardsworth, and Christina Rosetti.

518. *Rebecca of Sunnybrook Farm.* Boston: Houghton-Mifflin, 1903. The sentimental story of New England farm life with a heroine who faces harsh conditions, but remains full of hope. A children's classic.

519. *The Story Hour: A Book for Home and Kindergarten.* Boston: Houghton-Mifflin, 1910. A collection of stories for parents and teachers intended to teach young children.

520. *My Garden of Memory: An Autobiography.* Boston: Houghton-Mifflin, 1923. Provides insight into Wiggin and her translation of Froebel's philosophy into practice.

SECONDARY SOURCES

521. Smith, Nora Archibald. *Kate Douglas Wiggin as her Sister Knew Her.* Boston: Houghton-Mifflin, 1925. Provides the insights of a sibling who worked with Wiggin. Smith states that the book is not intended to be a biography, but to "fill the gaps in *My Garden of Memory*" (see no. 520). Discusses Wiggin's role as a teacher and teacher educator.

522. Snyder, Agnes. *Dauntless Women in Childhood Education, 1856-1931.* Washington, D.C.: Association for Childhood Education International, 1972, pp. 89-123. Provides biographical data and an analysis of Wiggin's contributions to the early years of the kindergarten movement with a discussion of her educational writings. Provides a brief comparison between Wiggin's writings and the writings of Susan Blow. No bibliography is provided, but the footnotes contain complete citations.

Appendix: A Chronological List

PRE-MODERN PIONEERS

Johann Amos Comenius (1592-1670)
John Locke (1632-1704)
Jean-Jacques Rousseau (1712-1778)
Johann Heinrich Pestalozzi (1746-1827)
Robert Owen (1771-1858)
Friedrich Wilhelm Froebel (1782-1852)

MODERN PIONEERS

Elizabeth Palmer Peabody (1804-1894)
Emma Jacobina Christiana Marwedel (1818-1893)
William Torrey Harris (1835-1908)
William Nicholas Hailmann (1836-1920)
Alice Harvey Whiting Putnam (1841-1919)
Susan E. Blow (1843-1916)
Granville Stanley Hall (1844-1924)
Elizabeth Harrison (1849-1927)
Lucy Craft Laney (1854-1933)
Kate Douglas Wiggin (1856-1923)
Lucy Wheelock (1857-1946)
John Dewey (1859-1952)
Rachel McMillan (1859-1917)
Margaret McMillan (1860-1931)
Mary Church Terrell (1863-1954)
Ella Victoria Dobbs (1866-1952)
Caroline Pratt (1867-1954)
Patty Smith Hill (1868-1946)
Maria Montessori (1870-1952)
William Heard Kilpatrick (1871-1965)
Alice Temple (1871-1946)
Edward Lee Thorndike (1874-1949)
Lucy Sprague Mitchell (1878-1967)
Arnold Lucius Gesell (1880-1961)
Abigail Adams Eliot (1892-1992)
Jean Piaget (1896-1980)
Amy M. Hostler (1898-1987)

Leland B. Jacobs (1907-1992)
Lillian Weber (1917-1994)
Evangeline H. Ward (1920-1985)

Bibliography

Barnard, Henry, ed. *Kindergarten and Child Culture Papers*. Hartford: Office of
   Barnard's American Journal of Education, 1980.
Beatty, Barbara. *Preschool Education in America. The Culture of Young Children
   from the Colonial Era to the Present*. New Haven: Yale University Press,
   1995.
Braun, Samuel J., and Edwards, Esther P. *History and Theory of Early Childhood
   Education*. Worthington, Ohio: Jones, 1972.
Cleverley, John, and Phillips, D. C. *Visions of Childhood. Influential Models from
   Locke to Spock*. New York: Teachers College Press, 1986.
Committee of Nineteen. *Pioneers of the Kindergarten in America*. New York:
   Century & Co., 1924.
Cremin, Lawrence A. *The Transformation of the Schools: Progressivism in Ameri-
   can Education 1876-1957*. New York: Knopf, 1961.
Curti, Merle. *The Social Ideas of American Educators*. Paterson, New Jersey:
   Littlefield Adams, 1959.
Elkind, David, ed. *Perspectives on Early Childhood Education: Growing with Young
   Children Toward the Twenty-First Century*. Washington, D.C.: National
   Education Association, 1991.
Frost, Ilse. *Preschool Education: A Historical and Critical Study*. New York:
   Macmillan, 1927.
Frost, Joe L., ed. *Early Childhood Education Revisited*. New York: Holt, Rinehart
   & Winston, 1968.
Gordon, Ira J., ed. *Early Childhood Education. The Seventy-First Yearbook of the
   National Society for the Study of Education Part II*. Chicago: University
   of Chicago Press, 1972.
Lazeerson, Marvin. "Urban Reform and the Schools: Kindergartens in Massachu-
   setts 1870-1915." *History of Education Quarterly* 11, no. 2 (Summer
   1971): 115-142.
McMillan, Margaret. *The Nursery School*. New York: Dutton, 1919.
Owen, Grace, ed. *Nursery School Education*. New York: Dutton, 1923.
Ross, Elizabeth Dale. *The Kindergarten Crusade: The Establishment of Preschool
   Education in the United States*. Athens: Ohio University Press, 1976.
Shapiro, Michael Steven. *Children's Garden. The Kindergarten Movement from
   Froebel to Dewey*. University Park: The Pennsylvania State University
   Press, 1983.
Vanderwalker, Nina C. *The Kindergarten in American Education*. New York:
   Macmillan, 1908.

Warren, Donald, ed. *American Teachers: Histories of a Profession at Work.* New
    York: Macmillan, 1989.
Weber, Evelyn. *The Kindergarten: Its Encounter with Educational Thought in
    America.* New York: Teachers College Press, 1969.
Weber, Evelyn. *Ideas Influencing Early Childhood Education: A Theoretical Analy-
    sis.* New York: Teachers College Press, 1984.

Index

About the Author

BARBARA RUTH PELTZMAN is an Associate Professor in the Division of Education, Notre Dame College, St. John's University. Her numerous articles have appeared in publications such as *Reading Instruction Journal*, *The Reading Teacher*, *Learning Disabilities News*, and *Research and Teaching in Developmental Education*. She is also the author of *Anna Freud: A Guide to Research* (1990). An internationally respected scholar and researcher, she has presented papers at conferences around the world, and is a Fellow of the College of Preceptors in Essex, England.

ISBN 0-313-30404-1

HARDCOVER BAR CODE